GROKKING
THE SPRING
BOOT
INTERVIEW

by Javin Paul @javinpaul

Table Of Contents

Overview   2

How to Prepare for Spring Boot Interviews?   8

Topics   11

Spring Core Framework   13

  1. What is the Spring framework? Why should Java
programmers use the Spring framework?   15

  2. What is the Dependency Injection design pattern?   16

  3. What is the Inversion of Control concept, how does Spring
support IOC?   16

  4. How do you configure Spring Framework?   18

  5. Can we use more than one configuration file for our Spring
project?   18

  6. What types of dependency injection are supported by
Spring Framework? When do you use Setter and Constructor
Injection, the pros and cons?   18

  7. Difference between the setter and constructor injection in
Spring?   19

  8. Difference between Factory Pattern and Dependency
Injection in Java?   21

  9. What are the different modules in spring?   21

  10. What is the difference between Spring MVC and Spring
core?   21

  11. What is AOP? How is it implemented in Spring?   22

  12. What is Advice in AOP?   23

  13. What are the joint Point and point cut?   23

  14. What is component scanning in Spring Framework?   23

Container, Dependency, and IOC   25

  1. What is dependency injection and what are the advantages
of using it?   26

  2. What is an interface and what are the advantages of
making use of them in Java?   27

3. What is an ApplicationContext in Spring? 28

4. How are you going to create a new instance of an ApplicationContext? 29

5. Can you describe the lifecycle of a Spring Bean in an ApplicationContext? 32

6. How are you going to create an ApplicationContext in an integration test? 33

7. What is the preferred way to close an application context? Does Spring Boot do this for you? 34

8. What is Dependency injection using Java configuration? 35

9. What is Dependency injection using annotations (@ Autowired)?–Component scanning, Stereotypes?–Scopes for Spring beans? 35

10. What is the default scope? 35

11. Are beans lazily or eagerly instantiated by default? How do you alter this behavior? 35

12. What is a property source? How would you use @ PropertySource? 36

13. What is a BeanFactoryPostProcessor and what is it used for? When is it invoked? 37

14. Why would you define a static @Bean method when creating your own BeanFactoryPostProcessor? 37

15. What is a PropertySourcesPlaceholderConfigurer used for? 38

16. What is a BeanPostProcessor and how is it different to a BeanFactoryPostProcessor? What do they do? When are they called? 38

17. What is an initialization method and how is it declared on a Spring bean? 38

18. What is a destroy method, how is it declared and when is it called? 39

19. Consider how you enable JSR-250 annotations like @ PostConstruct and @PreDestroy? When/how will they get called? 41

20. How else can you define an initialization or destruction method for a Spring bean? 41

21. What does component-scanning do? 42

22. What is the behavior of the annotation @Autowired with regards to field injection, constructor injection and method injection? 43

23. How does the @Qualifier annotation complement the use of @Autowired? 44

24. What is a proxy object and what are the two different types of proxies Spring can create? 46

25. What are the limitations of these proxies (per type)? 46

26. What is the power of a proxy object and where are the disadvantages? 47

27. What is the difference between @Autowired and @Inject annotation in Spring? 47

Spring Bean Lifecycle **49**

1. What is a bean in Spring Framework? 50

2. What is the default scope of bean in the Spring framework? 50

3. Do Spring singleton beans are thread- safe? 50

4. What is the difference between a singleton and prototype bean? 50

5: Explain the Spring Bean-LifeCycle? 51

6. What is Bean Factory, have you used XMLBeanFactory? 53

7. What is the difference between ApplicationContext and BeanFactory in Spring framework? 53

8. What does the @Bean annotation do in Spring? 54

9. What is the default bean id if you only use @Bean? 55

10. How can you override this? 56

11. Why are you not allowed to annotate a final class with @Configuration? 56

12. How do @Configuration annotated classes support singleton beans? 56

13. Why can't @Bean methods be final either? 56

14. How do you configure profiles? 57

15. What are possible use cases where they might be useful?
57

16. Can you use @Bean together with @Profile? 58

17. Can you use @Component together with @Profile
annotation? 58

18. How many profiles can you have? 59

19. How do you inject scalar/literal values into Spring beans?
59

20. What is @Value used for? 60

21. What is Spring Expression Language (SpEL for short)? 60

22. What is the Environment abstraction in Spring? 61

23. Where can properties in the environment come from? 61

24. What can you reference using SpEL? 61

25. What is the difference between $ and # in @Value
expressions? 62

Aspect Oriented Programming (AOP) **63**

1. What is the concept of AOP? 66

2. Which problem AOP solves? 66

3. What is a cross-cutting concern? 66

4. Can you name three typical cross-cutting concerns? 66

5. What two problems arise if you don't solve a cross-cutting
concern via AOP? 67

6. What is a pointcut, a join point, advice, an aspect, weaving?
67

7. How does Spring solve (implement) a cross-cutting
concern? 68

8. What are the two proxy-types used in Spring AOP? 69

9. What are the limitations of the two proxy-types used in
Spring AOP? 70

10. What visibility must Spring bean methods have to be
proxied using Spring AOP? 71

10. How many advice types do Spring support? Can you name
each one? 71

11. What are they used for?   72

12. Which types of advice you can use to try and catch exceptions?   73

13. What is the JoinPoint argument used for?   74

15. What is a ProceedingJoinPoint? Which advice type is it used with?   74

16. Can you name some popular Aspect-oriented programming libraries?   75

17. What are the different types of Weaving which is available in AOP?   76

Spring MVC   **77**

1. MVC is an abbreviation for a design pattern. What does it stand for and what is the idea behind it?   79

2. Do you need spring-mvc.jar in your classpath or is it part of spring-core?   80

3. What is the DispatcherServlet and what is it used for?   80

4. Is the DispatcherServlet instantiated via an application context?   81

5. What is the root application context in Spring MVC? How is it loaded?   81

6. What is the @Controller annotation used for? How can you create a controller without an annotation?   82

7. What is the ContextLoaderListener and what does it do?   82

8. What are you going to do in the web.xml? Where do you place it?   83

9. How is an incoming request mapped to a controller and mapped to a method?   83

10. What is the @RequestParam used for?   84

11. What are the differences between @RequestParam and @PathVariable?   85

12. What are some of the valid return types of a controller method?   86

13. What is a View and what's the idea behind supporting different types of View?   87

14. How is the right View chosen when it comes to the rendering phase? 87

15. What is the Model in Spring MVC Framework? 88

16. Why do you have access to the model in your View? Where does it come from? 88

17. What is the purpose of the session scope? 89

18. What is the default scope in the web context? 89

19. Why are controllers testable artifacts? 89

20. What does the InternalResourceViewResolver do? 90

21. What is Spring MVC? Can you explain How one request is processed? 90

22. What is the ViewResolver pattern? how it works in Spring MVC 91

23. Explain Spring MVC flow with a simple example like starting from Container receives a request and forward to your Java application? 91

24. If a user checked in CheckBox and got a validation error in other fields and then he unchecked the CheckBox, what would be the selection status in the command object in Spring MVC? How do you fix this issue? 95

25. What are the different implementations of the View interface you have used in Spring MVC? 95

26. What is the use of DispatcherServlet in Spring MVC? 96

27. What is the role of InternalResourceViewResolver in Spring MVC 96

28. Difference between @RequestParam and @PathVariable in Spring MVC? 98

29. Difference between @Component, @Service, @Controller, and @Repository annotations in Spring MVC? 100

REST **103**

1. What does REST stand for? 105

2. What is a resource? 105

3. What are safe REST operations? 105

4. What are idempotent operations? Why is idempotency important? 105

5. Is REST scalable and/or interoperable? 106

6. What are the advantages of the RestTemplate? 106

7. Which HTTP methods does REST use? 107

8. What is an HttpMessageConverter in Spring REST? 107

9. How to create a custom implementation of HttpMessageConverter to support a new type of request/ response? 108

10. Is REST normally stateless? 108

11. What does @RequestMapping annotation do? 108

12. Is @Controller a stereotype? Is @RestController a stereotype? 109

13. What is the difference between @Controller and @RestController? 110

14. When do you need @ResponseBody annotation in Spring MVC? 110

15. What does @PathVariable do in Spring MVC? Why is it useful in REST with Spring? 111

16. What is the HTTP status return code for a successful DELETE statement? 111

17. What does CRUD mean? 111

18. Where do you need @EnableWebMVC annotation? 112

19. When do you need @ResponseStatus annotation in Spring MVC? 112

20. Is REST secure? What can you do to secure it? 114

21. Does REST work with transport layer security (TLS)? 114

22. Do you need Spring MVC in your classpath for developing RESTful Web Service? 115

Spring Boot Intro **116**

1. What is Spring Boot? Why should you use it? 118

2. What is the advantage of using Spring Boot? 119

3. What is the difference between Spring Boot and Spring MVC? 119

4. What is the difference between Core Spring and Spring Boot? 120

5. What are some important features of using Spring Boot?120

6. What is auto-configuration in Spring boot? How does it help? Why is Spring Boot called opinionated? 122

7. What is starter dependency in Spring Boot? How does it help? 123

8. What is the difference between @SpringBootApplication and @EnableAutoConfiguration annotation? 123

9. What is Spring Initializer? why should you use it? 124

10. What is a Spring Actuator? What are its advantages? 125

11. What is Spring Boot CLI? What are its benefits? 126

12. Where do you define properties in Spring Boot application? 126

13. Can you change the port of the Embedded Tomcat server in Spring boot? If Yes, How? 127

14. What is the difference between an embedded container and a WAR? 128

15. What embedded containers does Spring Boot support? 128

16. What are some common Spring Boot annotations? 128

17. Can you name some common Spring Boot Starter POMs? 129

18. Can you control logging with Spring Boot? How? 129

19. Difference between @SpringBootApplication and @ EnableAutoConfiguration annotations in Spring Boot? 129

20. What is the difference between @ContextConfiguration and @SpringApplicationConfiguration in Spring Boot Testing? 130

21. Where does Spring Boot look for application.properties file by default? 130

22. How do you define profile specific property files? 130

Spring Boot Auto Configuration **132**

1. What is Spring Boot auto-configuration? 133

2. How does auto-configuration work? How does it know what to configure? 134

3. What are some common Spring Boot annotations? 134

4. What does @EnableAutoConfiguration annotation do? 142

5. How does Spring Boot auto-configuration works? 142

6. What does @SpringBootApplication do? 142

7. Does Spring Boot do component scanning? Where does it look by default? 145

8. How are DataSource and JdbcTemplate auto-configured? 145

9. What is the purpose of spring.factories? 146

10. How do you customize Spring Boot auto configuration? 147

11. How to create your own auto-configuration in Spring Boot? 147

12. What are the examples of @Conditional annotations? How are they used? 148

Spring Boot Starter **151**

1. What is starter dependency in Spring Boot? What is the advantage of it? 152

2. How do you define properties in Spring Boot? Where? 153

3. What does @SpringBootApplication annotation do? 154

4. What things affect what Spring Boot sets up? 154

5. What does spring boot starter web include? 155

6. Can you make your own custom starter dependency? 155

7. What are some common Spring Boot Starter dependencies? Can you name a few? 156

8. How do you add a Spring boot starter in your project? 156

9. Which Spring Boot starter will you add to enable Spring boot testing and relevant libraries? 157

10. What is Spring Boot Starter Parent? 157

Spring Boot Actuator **159**

1. What is the Spring Boot Actuator? 161

2. What are the different ways Actuator provides to gain insight into a Spring Boot application? 161

3. Why do you need to secure Spring Boot Actuator's endpoints? 162

4. How do you secure the Spring Boot Actuator's endpoint to restrict access? 162

5. What value does Spring Boot Actuator provide? 163

6. What are the two protocols you can use to access actuator endpoints? 163

7. What are the actuator endpoints that are provided out of the box? 163

8. What is the info endpoint for? How do you supply data? 164

9. How do you change the logging level of a package using the logger's endpoint? 165

10. How do you access an endpoint using a tag? 166

11. What are metrics for? 167

12. How do you create a custom metric? 167

13. What is a Health Indicator in Spring Boot? 168

14. What are the Health Indicators that are provided out of the box? 168

15. What is the Health Indicator status? 169

16. What are the Health Indicator statuses that are provided out of the box? 170

17. How do you change the Health Indicator status severity order? 170

Spring Boot CLI **172**

1. What is Spring Boot CLI? 173

2. Can you write a Spring application with Groovy? 174

3. What are the main advantages of the Spring Boot command-line interface (CLI)? 174

4. What does @Grab annotation do? When to use this? 174

5. What is Spring Initializer? 175

6. How does Spring Boot CLI resolve dependencies? 175

Spring Testing **177**

1. How to define a testing class in Spring? 179

2. Which starter package do you need to test the spring boot application? 180

3. What type of tests typically use Spring? 180

4. What are the three common Spring boot test annotations? 180

5. How can you create a shared application context in a JUnit integration test? 181

6. When and where do you use @Transactional in testing? 182

7. How are mock frameworks such as Mockito or EasyMock used in Spring Boot? 182

8. How is @ContextConfiguration used in Spring Boot? 183

9. How does Spring Boot simplify writing tests? 184

10. What does @SpringBootTest do? How does it interact with @SpringBootApplication and @SpringBootConfiguration? 185

11. When do you want to use @SpringBootTest annotation? 186

12. What does @SpringBootTest auto-configure? 187

13. What dependencies does the spring-boot-starter-test bring to the classpath? 187

14. How do you perform integration testing with @SpringBootTest for a web application? 187

15. When do you want to use @WebMvcTest? What does it auto-configure? 188

16. What are the differences between @MockBean and @Mock annotations? 188

17. When do you want @DataJpaTest for? What does it auto-configure? 189

18. What is the use of @DirtiesContext annotation while Testing Spring Boot application? 190

19. What is the difference between @ContextConfiguration and @SpringApplicatoinConfiguration in Spring Boot testing? 190

20. What is the difference between @ContextConfiguration and @SpringBootTest? 191

Data Management And JDBC   **193**

1. What is the difference between checked and unchecked exceptions?   194
2. Why does Spring prefer unchecked exceptions?   195
3. What is the Spring data access exception hierarchy?   195
4. How do you configure a DataSource in Spring?   196
5. What is the Template design pattern and what is the JDBC template?   197
6. What is a callback?   198
7. What are the JdbcTemplate callback interfaces that can be used with queries?   198
8. What is each used for? (You would not have to remember the interface names in the exam, but you should know what they do if you see them in a code sample).   199
9. Can you execute a plain SQL statement with the JDBC template?   200
10. When does the JDBC template acquire (and release) a connection, for every method called or once per template? Why?   201
11. How do the JdbcTemplate support queries?   201
12. How does it return objects and lists/maps of objects?   202
13. What is a transaction? What is the difference between a local and a global transaction?   203
14. Is a transaction a cross-cutting concern? How is it implemented by Spring?   204
15. How are you going to define a transaction in Spring?   204
16. What does @Transactional do?   204
17. What is the PlatformTransactionManager?   205
18. Is the JDBC template able to participate in an existing transaction?   206
19. What is @EnableTransactionManagement for?   206
20. How does transaction propagation work?   207

21. What happens if one @Transactional annotated method is calling another @Transactional annotated method inside the same object instance? 209

22. Where can the @Transactional annotation be used? 209

23. What is a typical usage if you put it at the class level? 210

24. What does declarative transaction management mean?· What is the default rollback policy? How can you override it? 210

25. What is the default rollback policy in a JUnit test, when you use the @RunWith(SpringJUnit4ClassRunner.class) in JUnit 4 or @ExtendWith(SpringExtension.class) in JUnit 5, and annotate your @Test annotated method with @ Transactional? 212

Spring Data JPA **214**

1. What is JPA? 216

2. What are some advantages of using JPA? 216

3. What is the Spring data repository? 217

4. What is the naming convention for finder methods in the Spring data repository interface? 217

5. Why is an interface not a class? 217

6. Can we perform actual tasks like access, persist, and manage data with JPA? 217

7. How can we create a custom repository in Spring data JPA? 218

8. What is PagingAndSortingRepository? 218

9. What is @Query used for? 218

10. Give an example of using @Query annotation with JPQL. 218

11. Can you name the different types of entity mapping. 219

12. Define entity and name the different properties of an entity. 219

13. What is PlatformTransactionManager? 220

14. How can we enable Spring Data JPA features? 220

15. Differentiate between findById() and getOne(). 220

16. Are you able to participate in a given transaction in Spring while working with JPA?   220

17. Which PlatformTransactionManager(s) can you use with JPA?   221

18. What do you have to configure to use JPA with Spring? How does Spring Boot make this easier?   221

19. How are Spring Data JPA Repositories implemented by Spring at runtime?   222

20. What type of transaction Management Spring support? 223

21. How do you call a stored procedure by using the Spring framework?   223

22. What do the JdbcTemplate and JmsTemplate class offer in Spring?   224

Spring Cloud   225

1. Explain Spring cloud? or, What is Spring Cloud?   227

2. What are the common features of Spring cloud?   227

3. Explain load balancing? or What is load balancing?   227

4. How load balancing is implemented in Spring cloud?   228

5. What is the meaning of Service registration and discovery?
                                                        228

6. What is Hystrix?   228

7. Explain Netflix feign? Or What is Netflix feign?   229

8. Why do we use Netflix feign?   229

9. What is the use of the Spring cloud bus?   229

10. What are the advantages of Spring cloud?   229

11. What is PCF?   230

12. What is the purpose of the Hystrix circuit breaker? 230

13. Name the services that provide service registration and discovery.   230

14. Give the benefits of Eureka and Zookeeper?   230

15. What is the major difference between Spring Cloud and Spring boot?   230

16. What are some common Spring cloud annotations?   231

Spring Security   **232**

1. Spring Security Basics Interview questions   **234**

1. What is Spring Security?   234

2. What is the delegating filter proxy in Spring Security?   235

3. What are some restrictions on using delegating filter proxy in Spring security?   236

4. Do Filter's life-cycle methods like init() and destroy() will be a delegate to the target bean by DelegatingFilterProxy?   237

5. Who manages the life-cycle of filter beans in Spring?   237

6. What is the security filter chain in Spring Security?   238

7. What are some predefined filters used by Spring Security? What are their functions and in which order they occurred?   239

8. Can you add custom filters in Spring security's filter chain?   239

9. How to implement a custom filter in Spring Security?   240

10. How to add a custom filter into the Spring Security filter chain?   240

11. Is security a cross-cutting concern? How is it implemented internally?   241

12. What does @ and # is used for in Spring Expression Language (EL)?   242

13. Which security annotations are allowed to use SpEL?   242

14. What is a security context in Spring?   242

2. Spring Security Authentication and Authorization Interview Questions   **243**

15. What are authentication and authorization? Which must come first?   243

16. What is a Principal in Spring Security?   244

17. Why do you need the intercept-url?   244

19. Is it enough to hide sections of my output (e.g. JSP-Page)?   246

20. What type of object is typically secured at the method level (think of its purpose, not its Java type).   246

21. In which order do you have to write multiple intercept-urls? 246

22. What do @Secured and @RolesAllowed do? What is the difference between them? 248

3. Spring Security Password Encoding questions **249**

23. Does Spring Security support password hashing? What is salting? 249

24. What is PasswordEncoder? 250

25. What are some implementations of 250

PasswordEncoder in Spring Security? 250

26. How do you control concurrent Sessions on Java web applications using Spring Security? 251

27. How do you set up LDAP Authentication using Spring Security? 252

28. How to implement Role-Based Access Control (RBAC) using Spring Security? 257

Conclusion **259**

Grokking the Spring Boot Interview
© 2021, Javin Paul

Version 1.0 - January 2021

Overview

Java Interviews are notoriously tough, not because they ask impossible algorithmic questions like Google or Amazon but because of the vast nature of Java API, Frameworks and Libraries. ! It's not enough for you to just know Java and expect that you will be able to clear Java Interviews.

To pass the Java Interviews, you should also know essential Java frameworks like Spring, Spring Boot, and Hibernate. In my previous book, Grokking the Java Interview, I touched upon essential core Java topics like Collections, Multithreading, and Java Fundamentals and in this book, I have shared common Spring Framework questions from Job interviews.

Spring Framework is the most popular and almost a standard framework for developing Java applications, both core java as well as Java web application which runs on servers like Tomcat.

Like Java, Spring Framework is also very vast and there are several sub-projects like Containers, Core Spring Concepts like IoC and Dependency Injection, Spring MVC, Spring Boot, Spring Data JPA, Testing, and miscellaneous Spring APIs.

This book touches base on all of them and has questions to test your knowledge about those topics. You can use these questions to revise those essential Spring concepts in quick time and you can also use these questions to explore Spring Framework and Spring Boot further.

This book is also useful for Java developers who are preparing for the Spring Professional Certification Exam as I have tried to answer most of the questions from the Official Spring Certification Exam guide. This means you can use this as a review study guide for your spring certification preparation as well.

I also have a spring certification practice test on Udemy where I have shared 250+ high quality questions on Spring Boot, and Spring Security and other spring certification topics. If you are preparing for Spring certification you can use that to build the speed and accuracy required to prepare for the exam.

Remember, Spring Professional certification is not easy as it requires 76% to pass the actual exam which is very hard in limited time, especially if you haven't practiced before. That's the reason many experienced Java and Spring developers fail to clear the exam in the first attempt.

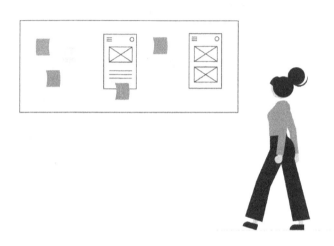

Why Prepare
For The Spring
Boot Interview?

Many Java developers, particularly experienced developers with a couple of years of experience think that it's not necessary to prepare for Java interviews, only to fluff their valuable chances. It doesn't matter how many years of experience you have in Java or Spring Boot, you must prepare for interviews.

Why? I suggest preparing because when you work on a vast technology like Java or Spring, you work on a particular area. It's almost impossible to learn all the areas of a particular framework. For example, if you are working in a Spring-based Java web application then you are expected to be better at Spring MVC and REST concepts but there is high-chance that you don't know much about other Spring concepts like Spring AOP or Spring Cloud.

And, believe it or not, interviews are almost always very different from real jobs. I don't know why but Interviewers expect you to know everything about Spring Framework, even if certain areas are never used in any project.

If your aim is to pass interviews because you desperately need the job then you don't have any choice, you cannot argue what is right or what is wrong, the best approach is to prepare hard and prepare well and that's where this book can help you.

While it's not possible to learn anything in a very short time, this book provides you a nice overview of almost all essential Spring concepts and you can easily finish the book in a few hours or few days.

If you are going for a Java Developer interview, where Spring and Spring Boot is mentioned as a desired skill then I highly recommend you to go through these questions before attending any telephonic or face-to-face interview. While there is no guarantee that the Interviewer will ask any question from this book, by going through the book, you already know most of the Spring concepts which you are expected to know.

How to Prepare
for Spring Boot
Interviews?

In order to best prepare for Spring Boot Interviews, you need to have a solid understanding of Spring Framework and their different sub-projects like Spring MVC, REST, Spring Data JPA, Testing, Spring Cloud etc.

If you have worked in Spring Boot projects then there is a good chance that you are already familiar with key concepts like auto-configuration, actuator, and starter dependencies. Those are must and if you haven't used them, I strongly suggest you to write a Spring boot program, or create a Spring boot project from scratch.

If you need help, you can find many Spring Boot projects on Youtube or you can join this Udemy course.

Once you have some experience under your belt, you can go through each topic and try to answer questions on your own. If you don't know, look at the answer and then research it to learn better. This is the best approach to prepare for the Spring boot interview but it requires time.

If you are short of time then there is no choice but to go through the question as soon as possible so that you can revise the essential concepts and at least have some idea about it.

Reviewing this book will not only help you gain both confidence and knowledge to answer the questions but more importantly it will allow you to drive the Java interview in your favor. This is the single most important tip I can give you as a Java developer.

Always, remember, your answers drive interviews, and these questions will empower you to drive the Interviewer to your stronger areas.

All the best for the Java interview and if you have any questions or feedback you can always contact me on Twitter at javinpaul or comment on my blogs Javarevisited and Java67.

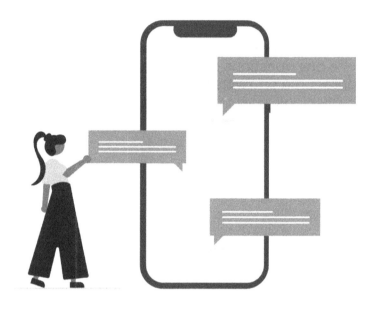

Topics

These are the topics which you need to prepare for Spring boot interviews:

1.   Core spring
2.   Container, Dependency Injections and IoC
3.   Spring Aspect-Oriented Programming
4.   Bean Life Cycle
5.   Spring MVC
6.   REST
7.   Spring Cloud
8.   Microservices
9.   Spring Data JPA
10. Spring Boot Testing
11. Spring Security
12. Spring Boot Core Concepts
13. Spring Boot Actuator

These are also the topics which you need to prepare for Spring Professional certification, which means you can kill two birds in one stone. I mean, by preparing for spring professional certification you can also get yourself ready for potential Spring Boot interviews and vice-versa.

That's actually the biggest benefit of any certification, the recognition part is great but the intangible benefit you get in terms of in-depth knowledge is far more valued, as it helps to clear potential Job interviews.

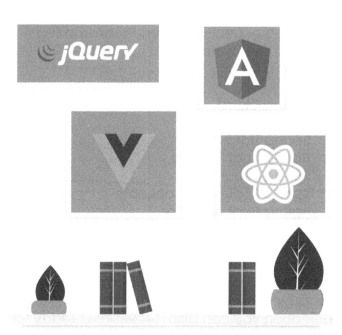

Spring Core Framework

Spring Interview Question is one of the first things Java programmers should prepare before appearing on any Java or Spring interview. With the immense popularity of Spring frameworks like Spring MVC and Spring Boot in the Java world, focus on Spring skills on interviews is increasing day by day.

For those who don't know, the Spring framework is one of the most popular structures for Java applications, which aims to simplify Java development. It revolutionized Java development when it initially came with concepts of Dependency Injection and Inversion of Control, which made writing testable and maintainable Java applications.

But the Spring framework just didn't stop there; it also provides useful API to Java programmers. The best thing is that Spring has kept evolving since its inception and addressing Java developers' concerns in different areas.

Spring framework is divided into many different modules like Spring MVC, Spring Integration, Spring Batch, Spring LDAP, Spring Security, Spring Boot, Spring Cloud, and several other modules, which focus on a particular area.

For example, Spring Boot tries to make it even easier to use the Spring framework by reducing the amount of configuration you need to put in for Spring itself. Spring Cloud is evolving to become the best framework for developing cloud-based Java frameworks and Microservices, which is a need for the future, and Spring Security has established itself as the go-to framework for security Java web applications.

Based on your work experience, the Interviewer can ask questions from core Spring or these modules.

That's why, while preparing the Spring interview question, focus on Spring core, Spring Security, and Spring API. These are main areas from where the interviewer asks questions.

If you have working experience in Spring- based Java projects, you can quickly answer most of these Spring questions from several Java interviews.

Now that you know the importance of Spring Framework for Java developers and ready to take on Spring questions on your next interview, let's see some frequently asked questions on the Spring framework on Java interviews:

Let's first start with the basics, in this section, you will see some Spring core interview questions focused upon what is Spring framework, how it works, what benefits it provides and dependency injection and inversion of control concepts.

1. What is the Spring framework? Why should Java programmers use the Spring framework?

Spring is a framework which helps Java programmers in development. In fact Spring is now the most popular Java Framework and most of the Java server side development are using Spring and other Spring projects like Spring Boot. At the very basic level, Spring Framework provides Dependency Injection and IOC containers, Spring MVC flow, and several useful API for Java programmers.

2. What is the Dependency Injection design pattern?

Java Programs involve a lot of object interaction. One object knows about other objects and requires them to function properly. Those objects are known as dependency and without them you cannot test your objects. Also, this interaction tightly couples different parts of application which means changing one part requires changes in multiple places. Dependency Injection is one of the design patterns, which allows injecting dependency on Objects, instead of object resolving the dependency.

3. What is the Inversion of Control concept, how does Spring support IOC?

The simple meaning of inversion of the control means that now the framework, Spring is responsible for creating objects, wiring dependencies, and managing their life-cycle instead of a developer, which was the case before. That's where control is inverted from

developer to framework.
In short, now we have inverted the control of creating the object from our own using a new operator to container or framework.

Now it's the responsibility of the container to create an object as required. We maintain one XML file where we configure our components, services, all the classes, and their property. We just need to mention which service is needed by which component and container will create the object for us.

This concept is known as dependency injection because all object dependency (resources) is injected into it by the framework.

Example:

```
<bean id="createNewStock"
      class="springexample.
stockMarket.CreateNewStockAccont">
      <property name="newBid"/>
   </bean>
```

In this example, `CreateNewStockAccont` class contains getter and setter for newBid and container will instantiate newBid and set the value automatically when it is used. This whole process is also called wiring in Spring and by using annotations it can be done automatically by Spring, referred to as auto-wiring of beans in Spring.

4. How do you configure Spring Framework?

Nowadays, Spring Framework is most configured using annotations and putting relevant JAR files in class files which is also done by Maven. Spring Boot takes configuration spring part away from Java developers by providing auto-configuration features which can automatically configure beans if certain JARs are present in classpath.

5. Can we use more than one configuration file for our Spring project?

Yes, you can use as many as you want, all you need to is import them in the main Spring configuration file which you will load from your program.

6. What types of dependency injection are supported by Spring Framework? When do you use Setter and Constructor Injection, the pros and cons?

There are 2 types of dependency injection supported by Spring, constructor based injection, and setter-based injection.

Both types have their own advantages and disadvantages; you should use Constructor injection when an object's dependencies are not optional, and they must be initialized with their dependencies.

Also, use constructor injection if the order of initialization or dependency matters because, in Setter based injection, you cannot impose any order. Use setter injection when dependencies are optional.

7. Difference between the setter and constructor injection in Spring?

Spring supports two types of dependency Injection, using a setter method, e.g. `setXXX()`, where XXX is a dependency or via a constructor argument. The first way of dependency injection is known as **setter injection** while later is known as **constructor injection**.

Both approaches of Injecting dependency on Spring bean has there pros and cons and here are key differences between them:

1. The fundamental difference between setter and constructor injection, as their name implies, is How dependency is injected. Setter injection in Spring uses setter methods like `setDependency()` to inject dependency on any bean managed by Spring's IOC container. On the other hand, constructor injection uses the constructor to inject dependency on any Spring-managed bean.

2. Because of using the setter method, setter Injection is more readable than constructor injection in Spring configuration files, usually `applicationContext.xml`. Since the setter

method has a name like `setReporotService()` by reading Spring XML config file you know which dependency you are setting. While in constructor injection, since it uses an index to inject the dependency, it's not as readable as setter injection and you need to refer to either Java documentation or code to find which index corresponds to which property.

3. Another difference between setter vs constructor injection in Spring and one of the drawbacks of setter injection is that it does not ensure dependency Injection. You can not guarantee that certain dependency is injected or not, which means you may have an object with incomplete dependency. On the other hand, constructor Injection does not allow you to construct an object until your dependencies are ready.

4. One more drawback of setter Injection is Security. By using setter injection, you can override certain dependencies which is not possible with constructor injection because every time you call the constructor, a new object is created.

5. Setter injection can also help to resolve circular dependency, for example, If Object A and B are dependent on each other i.e A is dependent on B and vice-versa. Spring throws `ObjectCurrentlyInCreationException` while creating objects of A and B bcz A object cannot be created until B is created and vice-versa.

So spring can resolve circular dependencies through setter-injection. Objects constructed before setter methods invoked.
In short, Setter injection is more flexible than constructor injection because you must remember the type and order of constructor parameters. Also, constructor injection is generally used to inject the mandatory dependency, while setter can be used to inject the optional dependency.

8. Difference between Factory Pattern and Dependency Injection in Java?

Even though both allow you to reduce coupling in code, dependency injection is much more flexible and easier to test than Factory pattern.

9. What are the different modules in spring?

Spring has seven core modules
1. The Core container module
2. Application context module
3. AOP module (Aspect Oriented Programming
4. JDBC abstraction and DAO module
5. O/R mapping integration module (Object/ Relational)
6. Web module
7. MVC framework module

10. What is the difference between Spring MVC and Spring core?

The Spring MVC is part of the Spring framework, which helps you to develop Java web applications using model web controller pattern, while Spring Core provides the Dependency injection and Inversion of Control. The Spring Container is part of Spring core.

Both functionalities come in different JAR files. If you are developing just a core Java application using Spring, then you just need Spring Core, but if you are developing a Web application, then you need spring-mvc.jar as well.

Now that we have seen some questions on Spring core and basics, it's time for Spring MVC interview questions which is probably the most important thing because of the popularity of Spring as an MVC framework and standard for developing Java web applications.

11. What is AOP? How is it implemented in Spring?

The core construct of AOP is the aspect, which encapsulates behaviors affecting multiple classes into reusable modules. AOP is a programming technique that allows a developer to modularize crosscutting concerns, that cuts across the typical divisions of responsibility, such as **logging and transaction management.**

Spring AOP, aspects are implemented using regular classes or regular classes annotated with the `@Aspect` annotation. In other words by using JDK Proxies or CGLib proxies.

12. What is Advice in AOP?

It's an implementation of an aspect; advice is inserted into an application at join points. Different types of advice include "around," "before" and "after" advice

13. What are the joint Point and point cut?

Similar to Object-oriented programming, AOP is another popular programming concept which complements OOP. A join point is an opportunity within the code for which we can apply an aspect. In Spring AOP, a join point always represents a method execution.

Pointcut: a predicate that matches join points. A pointcut is something that defines what join-points advice should be applied.

14. What is component scanning in Spring Framework?

This is one of the important features of Spring framework which helps in configuring your application. The process of searching the classpath for classes that should be part of the application context is called component scanning.

In order to do dependency injection, Spring creates a bean factory or application context when you start your spring application, Spring creates instances of objects and adds them to

the application context.
Objects in the application context are called "Spring beans" or "components". Spring resolves dependencies between Spring beans and injects Spring beans into other Spring beans' fields or constructors and it can do that by itself by using component scanning.

That's all about some of the core Spring Framework interview questions. These are the basics which every Java developer should know. To be honest, you will be really lucky if you get asked these kinds of questions in a real interview but they are important to understand Spring framework in general and require you to answer many of the Spring questions which you will see in this book.

Container,
Dependency,
and IOC

Now that we have seen some questions on Spring core and basics, it's time for Spring MVC interview questions which is probably the most important thing because of the popularity of Spring as an MVC framework and standard for developing Java web applications.

It was the dependency injection which made Spring framework popular in early 2000 as it made Java development much easier compared to J2EE. You can now test your code easily, particularly the web and DB layer which was hard to test earlier.

Spring Container is a very important concept to understand for both beginners and experienced Java developers as it's the core part of Spring and responsible for creating and managing Spring beans.

Now, let's jump to some frequently asked Spring interview questions on Container, Dependency and IOC. They are also good for spring certification.

1. What is dependency injection and what are the advantages of using it?

As the name suggests, Dependency injection means injecting the dependency on objects. If you know, an object works together, one object needs another to work and all the objects which it uses becomes its dependency, without them it cannot function.

This dependency tightly couples your code as these objects may be from different packages and modules. You may know that a tightly coupled system is hard to change as change in one part required change on other parts as well.

Dependency injection aims to solve this problem by injecting dependency at runtime, rather than object acquiring them. Since dependency is provided to an object, it's not really dependent on actual implementations, it can work as long as the object provided implements the interface. This makes testing really easy as you can provide mock or stub objects for testing.

Apart from testing and loosely coupled design, here are some more advantages of using dependency injection:

- Reduced glue boilerplate code, so code is cleaner.
- Decoupling is more effective (IOC containers support eager instantiation and lazy loading of services)
- Easier to test (no singletons or JNDI lookup mechanisms are required in unit tests)
- Better applications design with DI
- Increased module reusability and maintainability.
- Standardizes parts of application development

2. What is an interface and what are the advantages of making use of them in

Java?

An interface like a contract in Java. It promotes flexible coding which results in loosely coupled systems which are easier to change. If you remember, one of the common coding principles is *"code for interface rather than implementation"*, which means you should write your code using List rather than ArrayList.

When you do that, you can pass any kind of List like `Vector, ArrayList and LinkedList` and your code will function as expected.

Here are some more advantages of using interface in Java:

- You can provide different implementations at runtime,
- Allows you to inject dependencies, and
- Polymorphism.
- Using interfaces also makes testing easier as you can provide a mock or stub during the testing phase.

3. What is an ApplicationContext in Spring?

The `ApplicationContext` is the main interface within a Spring application that is used for providing configuration information to the application. It implements the `BeanFactory` interface.

It can also load bean definitions, wire beans together, and dispense beans upon request. Additionally, it adds more enterprise-specific functionality such as the ability to resolve textual messages from a properties file and the ability to publish application events to interested event listeners.

This container is defined by `org.springframework.context.ApplicationContext` interface. It represents the Spring IoC container and is responsible for instantiating, configuring, and assembling the beans.

4. How are you going to create a new instance of an ApplicationContext?

There are multiple ways to create an instance of ApplicationContext depending upon whether you are working in a core java application or a web application. For example, in core java applications,you can use `ClassPathXmlApplicationContext` to create instances of ApplicationContext. It looks for applicationContext.xml anywhere in the classpath (including JAR files).

Similarly, you can also use `FileSystemXmlApplicationContext` which looks for xxx.xml in a specific location within the filesystem, as well as `AnnotationConfigApplicationContext`, if you are using Java annotations to configure spring application. It is also the newest and most flexible implementation.

Here is an example of creating ApplicationContext instance using AnnotationConfigApplicationContext in Spring application:

```java
@Configuration
public class GreetingConfiguration{

  @Bean
  public GreetingProvider provider() {
    return new GreetingMessageProvider();
  }

  @Bean
  public GreetingRenderer renderer(){

    GreetingRenderer renderer = new
StandardOutMessageRenderer();
    renderer.setGreetingProvider(provider());
    return renderer;
  }
}

public class HelloWorldSpringAnnotated {

  public static void main(String[] args) {
    ApplicationContext ctx = new
AnnotationConfigApplicationContext
(GreetingConfiguration.class);
    MessageRenderer mr = ctx.getBean("renderer",
GreetingRenderer.class);

    mr.render();
  }
}
```

Similarly, in a spring based web application you can create an instance of ApplicationContext using `WebApplicationContext` which extends `ApplicationContext` and is designed to work with the standard javax.servlet.ServletContext so it's able to communicate with the container.

Here is an example of how to create instance of `ApplicationContext` in spring based web application using `AnnotationConfigWebApplicationContext`:

```java
public class BookServletContainerInitializer
implements ServletContainerInitializer {

  @Override
  public void onStartup(Set<Class<?>> c,
ServletContext ctx) throws ServletException {

    AnnotationConfigWebApplicationContext
applicationContext = new
AnnotationConfigWebApplicationContext();
    applicationContext.
register(BookConfiguration.class);

    DispatcherServlet dispatcherServlet = new
DispatcherServlet(applicationContext);

    ServletRegistration.Dynamic bookRegistration
= ctx.addServlet("book", dispatcherServlet);
    bookRegistration.setLoadOnStartup(1);
    bookRegistration.addMapping("/");
  }
}
```

5. Can you describe the lifecycle of a Spring Bean in an ApplicationContext?

Here is how lifecycle of a Spring bean looks in an `ApplicationContext`:

• Spring reads the bean configuration and metadata in the form of a `BeanDefinition` object is created for each bean.
• All instances of `BeanFactoryPostProcessor` are invoked in sequence and are allowed an opportunity to alter the bean metadata.

• After that, following steps are repeated for each bean in the container:

1. An instance of the bean is created using the bean metadata.
2. Properties and dependencies of the bean are set.
3. Any instances of `BeanPostProcessor` are given a chance to process the new bean instance before and after initialization.
4. Any methods in the bean implementation class annotated with `@PostConstruct` are invoked. This processing is performed by a `BeanPostProcessor`.

•   Any afterPropertiesSet method in a bean implementation class implementing the InitializingBean interface is invoked. This processing is performed by a `BeanPostProcessor`. If the same initialization method has already been invoked, it will not be invoked again.

- Any custom bean initialization method is invoked. Bean initialization methods can be specified either in the value of the init-method attribute in the corresponding <bean> element in a Spring XML configuration or in the initMethod property of the `@Bean` annotation. This processing is performed by a BeanPostProcessor. If the same initialization method has already been invoked, it will not be invoked again. Similarly, when the Spring application context is to shut down, the beans in it will receive destruction callbacks in this order:
- Any methods in the bean implementation class annotated with `@PreDestroy` are invoked.
- Any destroy method in a bean implementation class implementing the `DisposableBean interface is invoked. If the same destruct`ion method has already been invoked, it will not be invoked again.
- Any custom bean destruction method is invoked.

Bean destruction methods can be specified either in the value of the destroy-method attribute in the corresponding <bean> element in a Spring XML configuration or in the destroyMethod property of the `@Bean` annotation. If the same destruction method has already been invoked, it will not be invoked again.

6. How are you going to create an ApplicationContext in an integration

test?

You can use `@ContextConfiguration` annotation to define and `ApplicationContext` for your integration test as shown below:

```
@ExtendWith(SpringExtension.class)
@ContextConfiguration(classes=MyTestConfig.class)
public class MySpringAppTests {
@Autowired
private MyService testService;
}
```

It's worth noting that If you are using Junit version < 5 like JUnit 4 then you can also use `@RunWith(SpringRunner.class)` or @ RunWith(MockitoJUnitRunner.class) etc.
If you are using Junit version = 5, so you have to use `@ExtendWith(SpringExtension.class)` or @ `ExtendWith(MockitoExtension.class)` etc.

7. What is the preferred way to close an application context? Does Spring Boot do this for you?

When Spring application context is to shut down, the beans receive destruction callbacks in this order:

1. `@PreDestroy`
2. `destroy()` as defined by the DisposableBean callback interface
3. A custom configured `destroy()` method.

You can close application context in them.

However, Spring doesn't fire destruction callbacks automatically.

For web applications running as a servlet, you can simply call `destroy()` in the servlet `destroy()` method and for standalone Java applications you can use `AbstractApplicationContext`'s `registerShutdownHook()` method. The method automatically instructs Spring to register a shutdown hook of the underlying JVM runtime. After it is added, calls to `ctx.destroy()` or `close()` will be removed.
In the case of Spring Boot, It registers shutdown-hook that calls the `close()` method directly using the application context. This destroys all the beans, releases the locks, then closes the bean factory.

8. What is Dependency injection using Java configuration?

Singleton is the default scope for Spring beans.

9. What is Dependency injection using annotations (@Autowired)?–Component scanning, Stereotypes?–Scopes for Spring beans?

10. What is the default scope?

11. Are beans lazily or eagerly instantiated by default? How do you alter this

behavior?

By default, Spring beans are eagerly instantiated unless they are annotated to be initialized lazy using `@Lazy` annotation.

`ApplicationContext` implementations eagerly create and configure all singleton beans as part of the initialization process to avoid and detect all configuration errors immediately, as opposed to hours or even days later.

When this behavior is not desirable, you can prevent pre-instantiation of a singleton bean by marking the bean definition as being lazy-initialized. A lazy-initialized bean tells the IoC container to create a bean instance when it is first requested, rather than at startup

When a lazy-initialized bean is a dependency of a singleton bean that is not lazy-initialized, the `ApplicationContext` creates the lazy-initialized bean at startup, because it must satisfy the singleton's dependencies. The lazy-initialized bean is injected into a singleton bean elsewhere that is not lazy-initialized.

12. What is a property source? How would you use @PropertySource?

The property source is used to externalize your application properties into a property file. Also, PropertySource is an object representing a set of property pairs from a particular source and

@PropertySource is a convenient annotation for including properties to Spring's Environment and allowing to inject properties via @Value into class attributes. You can use @PropertySource together with @Configuration annotation.

13. What is a BeanFactoryPostProcessor and what is it used for? When is it invoked?

BeanFactoryPostProcessor is an interface and beans that implement it are actually beans that undergo the Spring lifecycle. A bean implementing BeanFactoryPostProcessor is called when all bean definitions will have been loaded, but no beans will have been instantiated yet. You can use BeanFactoryPostProcessor to change the bean definition.

14. Why would you define a static @ Bean method when creating your own BeanFactoryPostProcessor?

You may know that the static @Bean methods are called without creating their containing configuration class as an instance, which means you can use them for defining **postprocessor beans**, like BeanFactoryPostProcessor and BeanPostProcessor because such beans will get initialized early in the container lifecycle and should avoid triggering other parts of the configuration at that point.

Also worth noting is that calls to static @Bean

methods never get intercepted by the container, because CGLIB subclassing can override only non-static methods. This means, in static `@Bean` class, `@Autowired` and `@Value` do not work on the class itself, since it is being created as a bean instance too early.

15. What is a PropertySourcesPlaceholderConfigurer used for?

It is used by default to support the property-placeholder element in working against the spring-context-3.1 or higher XSD; whereas, spring-context versions <= 3.0 default to *PropertyPlaceholderConfigurer* to ensure backward compatibility.

16. What is a BeanPostProcessor and how is it different to a BeanFactoryPostProcessor? What do they do? When are they called?

`BeanFactoryPostProcessor` implementations are "called" during startup of the Spring context after all bean definitions will have been loaded but not initialized while `BeanPostProcessor` are "called" when the Spring IoC container instantiates a bean (i.e. during the startup for all the singleton and on demand for the prototypes one)

17. What is an initialization method and

how is it declared on a Spring bean?

The `@Bean` annotation supports specifying arbitrary initialization and destruction callback methods, much like Spring XML's init-method and destroy-method attributes to the bean element. You can use them to customize the initialization destruction process. We'll see this concept in more detail in the next question which is also related to this.

18. What is a destroy method, how is it declared and when is it called?

Spring not only provides you initialization and destroy method callbacks via InitializingBean and `DisposableBean` callback interfaces but also allows you to create custom `init()` and `destroy()` methods.

You can configure the Spring container to "look" for your custom `init()` and `destroy()` callback method names on every bean. The Spring IoC container calls that method when the bean is created and in accordance with the standard lifecycle callback contract .

This feature also enforces a consistent naming convention for initialization and destroy method callbacks.

Here is an example of custom `init()` and `destroy()` method in Spring

```java
public class CustomBookService implements
BookService {
    private BookDAO bookDao;

    public void setBookDAO(BookDAO bookDao) {
        this.bookDao = bookDao;
    }

    // this is the initialization callback
method
    public void init() {
        if (this.bookDao == null) {
            throw new IllegalStateException("The
[bookDao] property must be set.");
        }
    }

// this is the destroy callback method
  public void destroy() {
        if (this.blogDao != null) {
            this.bookDao = null;
        }
    }
}
```

If multiple lifecycle mechanisms are configured for the same bean then here are the order on which they are called:

1. Methods annotated with `@PostConstruct` are called first.

2. The `afterPropertiesSet()` as defined by the InitializingBean callback interface

3. A custom `init()` method

Similarly, Destroy methods are called in the same order:

1. Methods annotated with `@PreDestroy` annotation.

2. The `destroy()` as defined by the `DisposableBean` callback interface

3. A custom `destroy()` method

19. Consider how you enable JSR-250 annotations like @PostConstruct and @PreDestroy? When/how will they get called?

The JSR-250 `@PostConstruct` and `@PreDestroy` annotations are generally considered best practice for receiving lifecycle callbacks in a modern Spring application. Using these annotations means that your beans are not coupled to Spring-specific interfaces.

If you do not want to use the JSR-250 annotations but you still want to remove coupling, consider init-method and destroy-method bean definition metadata. These methods are called by Spring IoC containers as part of spring life-cycle. For example, `@PostConstruct` method is called after bean is created and `@PreDestroy` is called before bean is destroyed.

20. How else can you define an initialization or destruction method for a

Spring bean?

As we have seen in last 3 to 4 questions there are multiple ways to define and initialization or destruction method for a spring bean, for example the `org.springframework.beans.factory.InitializingBean` interface lets a bean perform initialization work after the container has set all necessary properties on the bean. The `InitializingBean` interface specifies a single method:

```
void afterPropertiesSet() throws
Exception;
```

The drawback of InitializingBean interface is that it unnecessarily couples the code to Spring.

21. What does component-scanning do?

Component-scanning is an important feature of Spring framework which helps in configuring your application. The process of searching the classpath for classes that should be part of the application context is called component scanning.

In order to do dependency injection, Spring creates a bean factory or application context when you start your spring application, Spring creates instances of objects and adds them to the application context.

Objects in the application context are called

"Spring beans" or "components". Spring resolves dependencies between Spring beans and injects Spring beans into other Spring beans' fields or constructors and it can do that by itself by using component scanning.

22. What is the behavior of the annotation @Autowired with regards to field injection, constructor injection and method injection?

Spring Framework allows three different types of dependency injections:

- **Constructor-based** dependency injection
- **Setter-based** dependency injection
- **Field-based** dependency injection

@Autowired annotation tries to find a matching bean **by type** and inject it at the place on annotation - that may be a constructor, a method (not only setter, but usually setter), and a field.

Here is how @Autowired finds the correct dependency to inject at runtime.

1. Spring Container examines the type of field
2. Container searches for a bean that matches the type
3. If multiple matching is found, `@Primary` bean is injected
4. If multiple matching is found, `@Qualifier` bean might be used

5. If multiple matching is found, try to **match bean name and filed name**
6. Spring will throw Exception if no unique matching is found

Another worth noting thing is that `@Autowired` **cannot** be used to autowire primitive values, or Strings. `@Value` specializes in this exactly. There are separate questions for that like the difference between `@Autowired` and `@Value` annotation.

Here is an example of `@Autowired` annotation in Spring:

```java
public class BookRecommendationEngine {

   private final ReaderPreferenceDao
readerPreferenceDao;

   @Autowired
   @Qualifier("primary")
   private BookCatalog bookCatalog;    //@Autowired
to fields

   @Autowired // to constructors
   public BookRecommendationEngine (@
Qualifier("secondary")ReaderPreferenceDao
readerPreferenceDao) {
      this.readerPreferenceDao =
readerPreferenceDao;
   }
}
```

23. How does the @Qualifier annotation complement the use of @Autowired?

There are situations when you create more than one bean of the same type and want to wire only one of them with a property. In such cases, you can use the @Qualifier annotation along with @Autowired to remove the ambiguity by specifying which exact bean should be wired.

For Example in following case it is necessary provide a qualifier

```
@Component
@Qualifier("author")
public Author implements Person {}

@Component
@Qualifier("publisher")
public Publisher implements Person {}


@Component
public Book {

    private Person person;

    @Autowired
    public Book(@Qualifier("author") Person
person){
        this.person = person;
    }

}
```

Note, If you are using field or setter injection then you have to place the @Autowired and @Qualifier on top of the field or setter function like show in above example, and If you are using constructor injection then the annotations should be placed on constructor, else the code would not work.

24. What is a proxy object and what are the two different types of proxies Spring can create?

The proxy represents the lazily-loaded object. The object itself, which might be loaded from a database, is not loaded until a method is invoked on its proxy. The proxy, which intercepts the method invocation, will then load the actual object into memory and delegate the method invocation to it.

Spring AOP uses either **JDK dynamic proxies** or **CGLIB** to create the proxy for a given target object. (JDK dynamic proxies are preferred whenever you have a choice). If the target object to be proxied implements at least one interface then a JDK dynamic proxy will be used but if target object doesn't implement any interface then CGLIB proxy is used because it can create a proxy using bytecode instrumentation.

25. What are the limitations of these proxies (per type)?

The main limitation of CGLIB proxies is that they can intercept only public method calls, which means *you cannot call non-public methods* on such a proxy. They are not delegated to the actual scoped target object.

The main limitation of JDK Proxy is that the scoped bean must *implement at least one interface* and that all collaborators into which the scoped bean is injected must reference the bean through one of its interfaces.

26. What is the power of a proxy object and where are the disadvantages?

Proxies are a great tool for adding functionality around beans methods. You can define some things to happen at different times around methods but you can also add new methods to beans by declaring new "parents" for the bean using `@DeclareParents` annotation.

Now, some disadvantage of proxies:

- Final methods cannot be advised, as they cannot be overridden

There is little performance difference between CGLIB proxying and dynamic proxies. Performance should not be a decisive consideration in this case.

27. What is the difference between @ Autowired and @Inject annotation in Spring?

The `@Autowired` annotation is used for auto-wiring in the Spring framework. If you don't know, autowiring is a process in which Spring framework figures out dependencies of a Spring bean, instead of you, a developer, explicitly specifying them in the application context file. You can annotate fields and constructor using `@Autowired` to tell Spring framework to find dependencies for you.

The `@Inject` annotation also serves the same purpose, but the main difference between them is that `@Inject` is a standard annotation for dependency injection and `@Autowired` is spring specific.

Since Spring is not the only framework which provides dependency injection, in the future if you change your container and moves to another DI framework like Google Guice, you need to reconfigure your application.

You can potentially avoid that development effort by using standard annotations specified by JSR-330 e.g. `@Inject, @Named, @Qualifier, @ Scope` and `@Singleton`.

A bean declared to be auto-wired using `@ Inject` will work in both Google Guice and Spring framework, and potentially any other DI container which supports JSR-330 annotations.
That's all about some frequently asked spring interview questions around Containers, dependency injection, and Inversion of Control. I have also tried to answer most of the questions from the Spring Certification guide. If you are preparing for Spring professional certification then you can review these questions to get some ideas and explore further.

Spring Bean Lifecycle

Now that we have seen some questions on Spring core and basics, it's time for Spring MVC interview questions which is probably the most important thing because of the popularity of Spring as an MVC framework and standard for developing Java web applications.

1. What is a bean in Spring Framework?

A bean is nothing but a Java class (POJO - Plain Old Java Object) whose life-cycle is managed by Spring framework. This means instances of bean are created, maintained and destroyed by Spring container.

2. What is the default scope of bean in the Spring framework?

The default scope of a Spring bean is the Singleton scope, and in the web application default scope of a spring bean in request scope. Singleton bean means the same instance of a bean is shared with all other beans, while request scope means a bean is alive only for a request.

3. Do Spring singleton beans are thread-safe?

No, Spring singleton beans are not thread-safe. Singleton doesn't mean bean would be thread-safe.

4. What is the difference between a singleton and prototype bean?

This is another popular *spring interview question* and an important concept to understand. Basically, a bean has scopes which define their existence on the application.

Singleton: means single bean definition to a single object instance per Spring IOC container.

Prototype: means a single bean definition to any number of object instances.

Whatever beans we define in the spring framework are singleton beans.

There is an attribute in bean tag named 'singleton' if specified true then bean becomes singleton and if set to false then the bean becomes a prototype bean. By default, it is set to true. So, all the beans in the spring framework are by default singleton beans.

```
<bean id="createNewStock" class="springexample.
stockMarket.CreateNewStockAccont"
     singleton="false">
        <property name="newBid"/>
  </bean>
```

5: Explain the Spring Bean-LifeCycle?

Ans: Spring framework is based on IOC so we call it an IOC container also So Spring beans reside inside the IOC container. Spring beans are nothing but Plain old Java objects (POJO).

Following steps explain their life cycle inside the container.

1. The container will look at the bean definition inside the configuration file (e.g. bean.xml).

2. Using a reflection container will create the object and if any property is defined inside the bean definition then it will also be set.

3. If the bean implements the `BeanNameAware` interface, the factory calls `setBeanName()` passing the bean's ID.

4. If the bean implements the BeanFactoryAware interface, the factory calls `setBeanFactory()`, passing an instance of itself.

5. If there are any BeanPostProcessors associated with the bean, their post-`ProcessBeforeInitialization()` methods will be called before the properties for the Bean are set.

6. If an `init()` method is specified for the bean, it will be called.

7. If the Bean class implements the DisposableBean interface, then the `destroy()` method will be called when the Application no longer needs the bean reference.

8. If the Bean definition in the Configuration file contains a 'destroy-method' attribute, then the corresponding method definition in the Bean

class will be called.

6. What is Bean Factory, have you used XMLBeanFactory?

Ans: `BeanFactory` is a factory Pattern which is based on IOC design principles.it is used to make a clear separation between application configuration and dependency from actual code. The `XmlBeanFactory` is one of the implementations of BeanFactory which we have used in our project.

The `org.springframework.beans.factory.xml.XmlBeanFactory` is used to create bean instances defined in our XML file.

```
BeanFactory factory = new XmlBeanFactory(new
FileInputStream("beans.xml"));
```

Or

```
ClassPathResource resource = new
ClassPathResource("beans.xml");
XmlBeanFactory factory = new
XmlBeanFactory(resource);
```

7. What is the difference between ApplicationContext and BeanFactory in Spring framework?

This one is a very popular Spring interview question and often asks in an entry-level interview. ApplicationContext is the preferred way of using spring because of the functionality provided by it and the interviewer wanted to check whether you are familiar with it or not.

ApplicationContext	BeanFactory
Here we can have more than one config files possible	In this only one config file or .xml file
Application contexts can publish events to beans that are registered as listeners	Don't support.
Support internationalization (I18N) messages	It's not
Support application life-cycle events, and validation.	Doesn't support.
Supports many enterprise services such as JNDI access, EJB integration, remoting	Doesn't support.

That's all about the difference between ApplicationContext and BeanFactory in Spring Framework.

8. What does the @Bean annotation do in Spring?

The @Bean is a method level annotation and is used to define methods which return Spring Bean. In other words, it tells Spring framework that this method will return an object that should be registered as a bean in the Spring application context.

The `@Bean` annotation together with the method are treated as a bean definition, and the method name becomes the bean id.

The body of the method contains logic to create a bean instance.

1. You can trigger autowiring without adding the `@Autowire` attribute into the `@Bean` annotation.
2. When you place the `@Qualifier` annotation together with the `@Autowired` and `@Bean` annotations, autowiring behavior turns into `byName` mode.

Here is an example of `@Bean` annotation in Spring application:

```
@Bean()
 public mySpringBean mySpringBeanDefaultId() {
     return new MySpringBean();
 }
```

9. What is the default bean id if you only use @Bean?

The method name is the default bean id if you only use `@Bean` annotation. For example, in above code the bean id will be `"mySpringBeanDefaultId"` as that's the name of the method which is annotated by `@Bean` annotation.

10. How can you override this?

You can override default bean id by using "`name`" or "`value`" parameter with @Bean annotation as show in below example:

```
@Bean(name="hellobean")
 public mySpringBean mySpringBeanDefaultId() {
     return new MySpringBean();
 }
```

11. Why are you not allowed to annotate a final class with @Configuration?

Java Configuration in Spring Framework requires CGLIB subclassing of each configuration class at runtime, if the class is final then it cannot be subclasses in Java. That's why `@Configuration` classes and their factory methods **must not** be marked as final or private

12. How do @Configuration annotated classes support singleton beans?

Singleton is the default scope.

13. Why can't @Bean methods be final either?

That's because the CGLib proxy cannot override a final method which is actually not possible in Java.

14. How do you configure profiles?

There are multiple ways to configure profiles in Spring applications like JVM argument, Environment API, PropertySource, and @Profile annotation.

The easiest way is to specify them as the - `Dspring.profiles.active` JVM argument value.

You can also set them in code using Environment API, which allows you to access many System properties.

Here is an example:

```
// Environment API
 AnnotationConfigApplicationContext ctx = new
AnnotationConfigApplicationContext();
 ctx.getEnvironment().setActiveProfiles("dev");
 // ctx.getEnvironment().setActiveProfiles("dev",
"uat"); //works with multi profiles
 ctx.register(SomeConfig.class,
StandaloneDataConfig.class, JndiDataConfig.class);
 ctx.refresh();
```

15. What are possible use cases where they might be useful?

Sometimes you need to define beans according to the runtime environment, for example some beans are only valid in Dev or Production environments. The `@Profile` are eligible for registration when one or more profiles are active. **Annotation Type Profile** allows for registering different beans depending on different conditions, for example, different dataSource configuration for different environments.

Another example is authorization which might be driven by different services in Dev, UAT vs Production environment. In these cases, having a different profile helps.

Here is an example of using @Profile annotation

```
@Configuration
@Profile({"dev", "qa"})
public class TestDataConfig {
    @Bean
    public DataSource dataSource() {
        return new EmbeddedDatabaseBuilder()
            .setType(EmbeddedDatabaseType.HSQL)
            .addScript("classpath:com/abc/config/
sql/schema.sql")
            .build();
    }
}
```

16. Can you use @Bean together with @Profile?

Yes, you can use @Profile annotation at @Bean methods level, you don't need two separate classes to work with two different databases. We can define two @Bean methods in the same class. Using this you can combine both Dev and Prod data source definitions into one class

17. Can you use @Component together

with @Profile annotation?

Yes, you can use @Component annotation together with @Profile in Spring. The @Profile annotation lets you indicate that a component is eligible for registration when one or more specified profiles are active.

Here is an example of using @Component with @Profile annotation:

```
@Configuration
@Profile({"dev", "qa"})
public class TestDataConfig {
    @Bean
    public DataSource dataSource() {
        return new EmbeddedDatabaseBuilder()
            .setType(EmbeddedDatabaseType.HSQL)
            .addScript("classpath:com/abc/config/
sql/schema.sql")
            .build();
    }
}
```

18. How many profiles can you have?

The short answer to this question is Integer. MAX_VALUE. If you are thinking why then just think that setActiveProfiles() method accepts String... varargs, which is a String[]. In Java, arrays internally use integers for index, the max size is Integer.MAX_VALUE. So theoretically it is 2^31-1 = 2147483647

19. How do you inject scalar/literal values

into Spring beans?

You can use `@Value` annotation to inject scaler or literal values into Spring beans. Since `@Autowired` cannot be used to autowire primitive values, or Strings, `@Value` is used . You can use `@Valu`e to insert scalar values or can be used together with placeholders and SpEL in order to provide flexibility in configuring a bean.

Here is an example:

```
@Component
public class HelloWorld{

  @Value("$appName}")
  private String name;

  public String getName() {
    return name;
  }

  public void setName(String name) {
    this.name = name; }
}
```

20. What is @Value used for?

The @Value is used to specify a default value for the affected argument. It is commonly used for injecting values into configuration variables -

21. What is Spring Expression Language (SpEL for short)?

The SpEL is an **expression language** that allows for querying and manipulating an object graph at runtime in Spring for example, ,@ `Value("#{myBean.someField}")`

22. What is the Environment abstraction in Spring?

The Environment is an abstraction integrated in the Spring container that models two key aspects of the application environment: profiles and properties.

The Spring `ApplicationContext` interface extends the EnvironmentCapable interface, which contains one single method namely the `getEnvironment()`, which returns an object implementing the Environment interface. Thus a Spring application context has a relation to one single Environment object.

23. Where can properties in the environment come from?

Properties in Spring application can come from a **variety of sources:**

- JVM system properties
- Operating system environment variables
- Command-line arguments
- Application property configuration files like application.properties or application.yml

24. What can you reference using SpEL?

Here are things you can refer following using SpEL in Spring :

- Static methods and static properties/fields
- Properties and methods in Spring beans: @ mybean.injectedValue
- Properties and methods in Java objects: #javaObject.firstName
- (JVM) System properties: @ systemProperties['os.name'
- System environment properties: @ systemEnvironment['JAVA_HOME'
- Spring application environment: @ environment['defaultProfiles'][0]

25. What is the difference between $ and # in @Value expressions?

The **$** is used to reference a property name in the application's environment. These are evaluated by the `PropertySourcesPlaceholderConfigurer` Spring bean prior to bean creation and can only be used in @Value annotations.

On the other hand, you can use # on Spring Expression language (SpEL) and can refer to many things like static methods or a field.

That's all about Spring Bean related interview questions and answers. I highly recommend you to revise these questions before going for a face-to-face or telephonic interview. You can also use them if you are preparing for spring certification as they answer most of the questions from the updated spring professional exam guide.

Aspect Oriented Programming (AOP)

If you are preparing for Java and Spring Developer interviews or Spring professional certification then a good knowledge of Aspect-oriented Programming or AOP is required. It's a boring and tough topic but very important from a Spring interview and Spring certification point of view and that's where these 13+ AOP interview questions will help you. I have sharing interview questions for Java developers on a regular basis and earlier I have shared spring boot interview questions and recently I shared spring cloud, spring data JPA, and Spring security questions, which are all important for both Spring developer's interview as well as spring certification point of view. In this article, I am going to share frequently asked AOP interview questions and also try to answer AOP questions given on the official Spring certification exam guide.

Aspect-Oriented Programming is a powerful technique to alter the behavior of your code to address the cross-cutting concern. You might be thinking about what is a cross-cutting concern and how one can alter the behavior of your code, well it's not intuitive but it's possible.

To be honest, AOP is a boring concept, at least for me, when I first read about AOP I didn't get it at all. I was lost in AOP jargons like Advice, JoinPoint, Pointcut, Weaving, and whatnot. It's only when I read the Spring in Action book and followed its Electric meter example, I was able to understand Aspect-Oriented Programming.

I found that Aspect-oriented programming solves some problems which are not easier to solve by Object-oriented programming. It's not that you can't solve them using OOP but they are not elegant.

In order to understand AOP, you need to understand a thing called cross-cutting concern, they are nothing but non-functional requirements which are used at multiple layers of your application. For example, logging is a cross-cutting concern as you need logging everywhere in your application. Similarly, security is a cross-cutting concern which requires multiple places in your application.

You can easily use Inheritance or Delegation to solve those problems i.e. define a class which does logging and security and let your business object implement them but that would make your business classes complex and cluttered. Aspect oriented programming solves those problems by inserting code for those cross-cutting patterns without you knowing about it.

For example, AOP can insert code at compile-time or when your class is loaded, or even when your methods are called. Those are actually called weaving and different AOP libraries have different weaving capabilities. For example, a powerful AOP library like AspectJ can change the bytecode while a less powerful Spring AOP can use a proxy object to implement those crossing-cutting concerns.

Without wasting any more of your time, let's jump into the boring world of AOP with some frequently asked AOP questions. I have tried to answer my best but if you want to learn more, I always suggest reading my favorite book Spring in Action by Craig walls, the best resources for any spring developer.

1. What is the concept of AOP?

AOP stands for Aspect-Oriented Programming and it helps decouple cross-cutting concerns from the object that they affect. It's similar to DI in the sense that DI helps decouple an application's object from each other.

2. Which problem AOP solves?

AOP helps in separating cross-cutting concerns from the business logic, which results in cleaner code and also helps developers to focus on building business logic.

3. What is a cross-cutting concern?

The cross-cutting concern is common functionality that is scattered around multiple places. They are common and you aspect they should be structured but they are not, which makes them hard to manage. AOP helps them to manage the cross-cutting concerns.

4. Can you name three typical cross-cutting concerns?

There are many cross-cutting concerns but the three most common ones are logging, security, and caching.

5. What two problems arise if you don't solve a cross-cutting concern via AOP?

It will make your code clutters as concerns will be spread across your application, which will be hard to manage.

6. What is a pointcut, a join point, advice, an aspect, weaving?

These are common AOP terms that every programmer needs to know as you just cannot work in AOP without knowing these terms. They are the backbone of AOP but at the same time they are not intuitive and boring and hard to understand, anyway, let's try to learn them.

1. Aspect

An aspect is a common feature that's typically scattered across methods, classes, object hierarchies, or even entire object models.

2. Advice

This is the functionality that is applied using AOP. It defines the "what" and "when" part of the aspect.

3. JoinPoint

These are the places where you can apply your "advice". There can be multiple join points in the flow of a program

4. Pointcut

They are used to find the join points where advice needs to be applied. You can define Pointcut by class name or method name, or you can use regular expressions to find different join points to apply your advice.

5. Weaving

This is a process of applying aspects to a target object to create a new proxied object. In simple words, it's a process when the AOP library or framework adds dynamic code to alter the behavior of your program. For example, compile-time weaving can add new code at compile time.

7. How does Spring solve (implement) a cross-cutting concern?

Spring uses proxy objects to implement the method invocation interception part of Aspect-Oriented Programming. Such proxy objects wrap the original Spring bean and intercept method invocations as specified by the set of pointcuts defined by the cross-cutting concern.

This means when you call a method on a spring bean, the method on a proxy object is called which extends the original spring bean. It then does whatever it has to do as part of implementing cross-cutting concerns like logging or security check and then calls the original method.

8. What are the two proxy-types used in Spring AOP?

There are two dynamic proxy techniques used in spring AOP, JDK dynamic proxy and CGLIB proxy

1. JDK dynamic proxy

In the case of JDK dynamic proxy, Proxies are created at runtime by generating a class that implements all the interfaces that the target object implements. Since standard Java features are used, no additional libraries are required. It's also worth noting that JDK dynamic proxies are the default proxy mechanism used by Spring AOP.

2. CGLIB proxy

This is another way to generate Proxy objects in Spring, it requires a third-party library called CGLIB which is included in the spring-core JAR. CGLIB proxies are created by generating a subclass of the class implementing the target object.

he CGLIB proxy mechanism will be used by Spring AOP when the Spring bean for which to create a proxy does not implement any interfaces. It is also possible to instruct Spring AOP to use CGLIB proxies by default using annotation `@EnableAspectJAutoProxy(proxyTargetClass = true)`

Another worth noting is that Spring Java configuration classes, annotated with `@Configuration`, will always be proxied using CGLIB.

9. What are the limitations of the two proxy-types used in Spring AOP?

As stated in the last question, Spring AOP uses JDK proxy and CGLIB proxies and both proxy objects have the same limitation: the invocation of advised methods on self.

If a method in the proxy calls another method in the proxy, and both match the pointcut expression of advice, the advice will be executed only for the first method. This is the proxy's nature: it executes the extra behavior only when the caller calls the target method.

Apart from that here are some more limitation of each proxy types:

JDK Dynamic Proxies Limitations

- Your target object must implement an interface.
- Only public methods will be proxied.

- Any methods found in the target object but not in any interface implemented by the target object cannot be proxied.
- Aspects can be applied only to Spring Beans. That means even if Spring AOP is not set to use CGLIB proxies if a Join Point is in a class that does not implement an interface, Spring AOP will try to create a CGLIB proxy.

CGLIB Proxy Limitations

- Class and Methods cannot be final
- Only public and protected methods can be proxied.
- It takes more time to create a proxy object, although it has better performance

That's all about the difference between JDK proxies and CGLIB proxies and their limitations.

10. What visibility must Spring bean methods have to be proxied using Spring AOP?

Only public methods of Spring beans will be proxied Additionally the call to the public method must originate from outside of the Spring bean.

10. How many advice types do Spring support? Can you name each one?

Spring Aspects can work with five types of advice:

@Before

This advice functionality takes place before the advised method is invoked.

@After

The advice functionality takes place after the advised method completes
@AfterReturning

This advice functionality is implemented after the advised method successfully completes.
@AfterThrowing

This advice functionality is implemented after the advised method throws an Exception

@Around

This advice wrap the advised method, provided some functionality before and after the advised method is invoked

11. What are they used for?

Now that you know different types of advice you can actually think where can they be used, nonetheless here are some points

@Before

Since before advice always proceed to the join point unless execution is thrown from within the advice code you can use this for Access control, security, and Statistics

@AfterReturning

In this advice functionality takes place after the execution of a join point has completed without throwing any exceptions and you can use this for statistics and Data validation
@AfterThrowing

This is invoked after the execution of a join point that resulted in an exception being thrown Error handling you can use this to send alerts to your monitoring tools when an error has occurred as well for error recovery.

@After

This advice will execute after a join point execution, no matter how the execution ends (even exception happens). You can use this for releasing resources just like the final clause in Java.

@Around

This is multi-purpose advice and can be used for all of the use-cases for AOP.

12. Which types of advice you can use to try and catch exceptions?

You can use both `@Around` and `@AfterThrowing` advice in this case but only `@Around` advice allows you to catch exceptions in the advice that occur during the execution of a join point.

13. What is the JoinPoint argument used for?

A JoinPoint argument can be used to retrieve additional information about the join point during execution. If used, JoinPoint needs to be the first parameter of Advice, only, in that case, Spring Framework will inject JoinPoint into the advice method.

JoinPoint is supported in `@Before`, `@After`, `@AfterReturning`, and `@AfterThrowing` advice and you can use JointPoint different kinds of information like:

- The string representation of JoinPoint
- Arguments of JoinPoint (for example Method Arguments)
- Signature of JoinPoint (for example Method Signature)
- Type of JoinPoint
- Target object being proxied

15. What is a ProceedingJoinPoint? Which advice type is it used with?

The `ProceedingJoinPoint` class is a parameter to `@Around` advice. When used it should be the first parameter of a method implementing an around advice.

When it's ready to pass control to the advised method, it will call `ProceedingJoinPoint`'s `proceed()` method, which is used to execute the actual method.

Here is an example of using `ProceedingJoinPoint` advice:

```
@Aspect
public class Book {

  @Pointcut("execution(** libary.Book.
read(..))")
  public void read() {}

  @Around("read()")
  public void sitAndRead(ProceedingJoinPoint jp)
{
    try {
      System.out.println("sit down and relax");
      jp.proceed(); //this is important, you
must call proceed on ProceedingJoinPoint
    } catch (Throwable e) {
      System.out.println("sorry, other time");
    }
  }
}
```

16. Can you name some popular Aspect-oriented programming libraries?

Here is a list of some of the popular AOP libraries you can use to implement AOP in your application:

1. AspectJ
2. JBoss AOP
3. Spring AOP

17. What are the different types of Weaving which is available in AOP?

There are many types of weaving available in different AOP libraries like compile-time weaving, weaving at the time of class loading, or weaving when the method gets called.
That's all about the frequently asked Spring AOP Interview Questions. While Spring AOP is not a very popular topic on Java and Spring Boot interviews, it's very important for anyone who wants to master the spring framework.

AOP plays an important part in the Spring framework and it will help you understand how the Spring framework works behind the scene. If you want to understand the magic of Spring Framework and Spring Boot, learning Spring AOP will be key.

Spring MVC

Now that we have seen some questions on Spring core and basics, it's time for Spring MVC interview questions which is probably the most important thing because of the popularity of Spring as an MVC framework and standard for developing Java web applications.

The Spring MVC framework is one of the most popular Java frameworks for developing web applications. If you have been working in Java and the developing web-based application then there is a good chance that you have already used Spring MVC in your project.

In the last decade, it has become the de facto framework for developing Java web applications. Spring MVC is based on classic MVC (Model-View-Controller) design pattern but it is much more than that. It leverages Spring framework's strength in terms of dependency injection and Inversion of control and promotes loosely coupled architecture, similar to the Spring framework itself. Because of its immense popularity and usefulness, most of the Java development job requires a good knowledge of Spring and Spring MVC.

There is a lot of demand for a good Java developer with good knowledge and experience in Spring and Spring MVC. One way to prepare yourself for such job interviews is to look for good interview questions.

These questions not only help you to prepare well for interviews but also help you to understand the fundamental concepts better and encourage you to learn more by exploring and that's why I am always in search of good Spring MVC Interview questions.

Recently I was preparing for Spring Core Professional Certification when I came across some Spring certification guides from Pivotal. These guides contain some interesting questions on Spring MVC.

Even though these questions are provided just to give you an idea about the syllabus of Spring certification, I actually found many of such questions have already been asked to myself and friends in various Spring job interviews.

On request to a couple of my friends, I thought to share answers to these questions here. So, if you are preparing for either Spring Certification or Java Web Developer interview, you will find this list of Spring MVC Interview Questions very useful for your preparation.

1. MVC is an abbreviation for a design pattern. What does it stand for and what is the idea behind it?

MVC is an abbreviation for the Model-View-Controller design pattern. This pattern is based upon the separation-of-concerns design principle which promotes handling different functionality at different layers and loose coupling between layers.

In MVC pattern, the Model contains the data which is rendered by View and Controller to help in request processing and routing.
Neither Model knows about View, nor View is dependent upon Model, which means the same model can be rendered by different views e.g. JSP, FreeMarker or it can even be written as JSON or XML in case of RESTful Web Services

2. Do you need spring-mvc.jar in your classpath or is it part of spring-core?

The spring-mvc.jar is not part of spring-core, which means if you want to use the Spring MVC framework in your Java project, you must include `spring-mvc.jar` in your application's classpath. In Java web applications, `spring-mvc.jar` is usually placed inside /`WEB-INF`/lib folder.

3. What is the DispatcherServlet and what is it used for?

The DispatcherServlet is an implementation of Front Controller design pattern which handles all incoming web requests to a Spring MVC application. A Front Controller pattern (see Enterprise application design pattern) is a common pattern in web applications whose job is to receive all requests and route it to different components of the application for actual processing.

In the case of Spring MVC, DispatcherServlet routes web requests to Spring MVC controllers.

In Spring MVC, DispatcherServlet is used for finding the correct Controller to process a request, which it does with the help of handler mapping like @RequestMapping annotation.

It is also responsible for delegating logical view names to ViewResolver and then sending the rendered response to the client.

4. Is the DispatcherServlet instantiated via an application context?

No, DispatcherServlet is instantiated by Servlet containers like Tomcat or Jetty. You must define DispatcherServlet into the web.xml file.

You can see that the load-on-startup tag is 1 which means DispatcherServlet is instantiated when you deploy Spring MVC application to Tomcat or any other servlet container. During instantiation, it looks for a file servlet-name-context.xml and then initializes beans defined in this file.

5. What is the root application context in Spring MVC? How is it loaded?

In Spring MVC, the context loaded using `ContextLoaderListener` is called the "root" application context which belongs to the whole application while the one initialized using `DispatcherServlet` is actually specific to that servlet.

Technically, Spring MVC allows multiple `DispatcherServlet` in a Spring MVC web application and so multiple such contexts each specific for respective servlet but having the same root context may exist.

6.What is the @Controller annotation used for? How can you create a controller without an annotation?

The `@Controller` is a Spring MVC annotation to define Controller but in reality, it's just a stereotype annotation. You can even create a controller without `@Controller` by annotating the Spring MVC Controller classes using `@Component` annotation. The real job of request mapping to the handler method is done using `@RequestMapping` annotation.

7. What is the ContextLoaderListener and what does it do?

The `ContextLoaderListener` is a listener which helps to bootstrap Spring MVC. As the name suggests it loads and creates `ApplicationContext`, so you don't have to write explicit code to create it.

The application context is where Spring bean leaves. For a Web application, there is a subclass called `WebAppliationContext`.

The ContextLoaderListener also ties the lifecycle of the ApplicationContext to the lifecycle of the

ServletContext. You can get the ServletContext from WebApplicationContext using the getServletContext() method.

8. What are you going to do in the web. xml? Where do you place it?

The ContextLoaderListener is configured in web.xml as listener and you put that inside a tag as shown below:

```
<listener>
<listener-class>
    org.springframework.web.context.
ContextLoaderListener
</listener-class>
</listener>
```

When the Spring MVC web application is deployed, Servlet container creates an instance of ContextLoaderListener class which loads the Spring's WebApplicationContext.

9. How is an incoming request mapped to a controller and mapped to a method?

Sometimes this question is also asked How does DispatcherServlet know which Controller should process the request? Well, the answer lies in something called handler mappings.

Spring uses handler mappings to associate controllers with requests, two of the commonly used handler mappings

are `BeanNameUrlHandlerMapping` and `SimpleUrlHandlerMapping`.
In `BeanNameUrlHandlerMapping`, when the request url matches the name of the bean, the class in the bean definition is the controller that will handle the request.

On the other hand, In `SimpleUrlHandlerMapping`, the mapping is more explicit. You can specify the number of URLs and each URL can be explicitly associated with a controller.

Btw, if you are using annotations to configure Spring MVC, which you should then @ `RequestMapping` annotations are used to map an incoming request to a controller and a handler method.

You can also configure `@RequestMapping` annotation by URI Path, by query parameters, by HTTP methods of a request and by HTTP headers present in the request.

10. What is the @RequestParam used for?

The `@RequestParam` is a Spring MVC annotation which is used to extract request parameter or query parameters from URL in Controller's handler method as shown below:

```
public String personDetail(@RequestParam("id")
long id){

   ....
   return "personDetails";
}
```

The `@RequestParam` annotation also supports data type conversion e.g. you can see here a String is converted to long automatically but it can also result in an exception if the query parameter is not present or in case of a type mismatch. You can also make the parameter optional by using required=false like `@RequestParam(value="id", required=false )`

11. What are the differences between @RequestParam and @PathVariable?

Even though both `@RequestParam` and `@PathVariable` annotations are used to extract some data from the URL, there is a key difference between them.

The `@RequestParam` is used to extract query parameters e.g. anything after "?" in URL while `@PathVariable` is used to extract the part of the URI itself. For example, if the given URL is `http://localhost:8080/SpringMVC/books/3232233/?format=json`

Then you can access the query parameter "format" using `@RequestParam` annotation and /books/{id} using `@PathVariable`, which will give you 3232233.

Here is another example of `@PathVariable`,

```
@RequestMapping ("/persons/{id}" )
public String personDetail (@PathVariable ("id"
) long id) {
    // functional code
}
```

This code can extract person id=123 from /persons/123. It is particularly used in RESTful Web Services because their id is usually part of the URI or URL path.

12. What are some of the valid return types of a controller method?

There are many return types available for a controller method in Spring MVC which is annotated by `@RequestMapping` inside the controller. Some of the popular ones are:

1. String
2. void
3. View
4. ModelAndView (Class)
5. Model (Interface)
6. Map
7. HttpEntity<?> or ResponseEntity<?>
8. HTTP headers

You can see the full list of valid return types for a Spring MVC controller here. http://docs.spring. io/spring/docs/current/spring-framework-reference/htmlsingle/#mvc-ann-return-types

Every return type has its specific use. For example, if you are using String then it means Controller just returns view name and this view name will resolve by `ViewResolver`.

If you don't want to return any view name, mention return type void. If you want to set view name as well as want to send some object use `ModelAndView` as a return type.

13. What is a View and what's the idea behind supporting different types of View?

A View is an interface in Spring MVC application whose implementations are responsible for rendering context and exposing the model. A single view exposes multiple model attributes. Views in Spring MVC can be beans also.

They are likely to be instantiated as beans by a `ViewResolver`. As this interface is stateless, view implementations should be thread-safe. by using `ViewResolver`, a logical name of view can be resolved into different types of View implementation e.g. `JstlView` for displaying JSP or other view implementations for `FreeMarker` and `Velocity`.

14. How is the right View chosen when it comes to the rendering phase?

The right View is chosen by ViewResolver in Spring MVC. When the Controller returns a logical view name to `DispatcherServlet`, it consults ViewResolver to find the right View.

The `ViewResolver` depending upon its implementation resolves the logical view into a physical resource e.g. a JSP page or a FreeMarker template.
For example, InternalResourceViewResolver is a default view resolver which converts logical view name e.g. "hello" to "/WEB-INF/`hello.jsp`" using prefix and suffix.

15. What is the Model in Spring MVC Framework?

The model is again a reference to encapsulate data or output for rendering. The model is always created and passed to the view in Spring MVC. If a mapped controller method has a Model as a method parameter, then a model instance is automatically injected by the Spring framework to that method.

Any attributes set on the injected model are preserved and passed to the View. Here is an example of using Model in Spring MVC:

```
public String personDetail(Model model) {
...
model.addAttribute("name", "Joe");
...
}
```

16. Why do you have access to the model

in your View? Where does it come from?

You need to have access to the model in your View to render the output. It's the model that contains the data to be rendered. The Model comes with the Controller, which processes their client request and encapsulates the output into a Model object.

17. What is the purpose of the session scope?

The purpose of the session scope is to create an instance of the bean for an HTTP Session. This means the same bean can serve multiple requests if it is scoped in session. You can define the scope of a Spring bean using scope attribute or `@Scope` annotation in Spring MVC application.

18. What is the default scope in the web context?

The singleton scope is the default scope for a Spring bean even in the web context. The other three Web context-aware scopes are a request, session, and global-session, which are only available in a web application-aware `ApplicationContext` object.

19. Why are controllers testable artifacts?

In Spring MVC Controllers are testable artifacts because they are not directly coupled with any View technology. They just return a logical view name, which can be easily tested.

20. What does the InternalResourceViewResolver do?

In Spring MVC, A `ViewResolver` returns View to handle output rendering based on the Logical View Name (provided by the controller) and locale. This way the controller is not coupled to specific view technology like JSP or `FreeMarker`; it only returns the logical view name.

InternalResourceViewResolver is the default View resolver configured in Spring MVC and DispatcherServlet uses it to find the correct view. InternalResourceViewResolver is used to render JSPs (JstlView).

It Configures prefix and suffix to logical view name which then results in a path to specific JSP as shown below:

```
<bean class= "org.springframework.web.servlet.
view.InternalResourceViewResolver" >
<property name= "prefix" value= "/WEB-INF/" />
<property name ="suffix" value =".jsp" />
</bean>
```

So if Controller returns "hello" as a logical view name, the InternalViewResolver will return /`WEB-INF/hello.jsp` and `DispatcherServlet` will forward the request to this JSP page for rendering.

21. What is Spring MVC? Can you explain How one request is processed?

Spring MVC is a framework to develop Java web applications. It provides an implementation of MVC or Model View Controller architecture, which is built on the separation of concerns and makes the development of Java web applications easy. In order to use this in your project, you need to learn Spring and include its JAR file.

22. What is the ViewResolver pattern? how it works in Spring MVC

View Resolver pattern is a J2EE pattern that allows a web application to dynamically choose its view technology, like HTML, JSP, Tapestry, JSF, XSLT, or any other view technology.

In this pattern, View resolver holds a mapping of different views, controller return name of the view, which is then passed to View Resolver for selecting an appropriate view.

23. Explain Spring MVC flow with a simple example like starting from Container receives a request and forward to your Java application?

It all starts with the client, which sends a request to a specific URL. When that request hits the web container like Tomcat it looks into web.xml and finds the Servlet or Filter which is mapped to that particular URL. It delegates that Servlet or Filter to process the request. Since Spring MVC is built on top of Servlet, this is also the initial flow of request in any Spring MVC based Java web application.

Remember, Web containers like Tomcat are responsible for creating Servlet and Filter instances and invoking their various life-cycle methods like `init()`, `service()`, `destroy()`. In the case of an HTTP request, HttpServlet handles that, and depending upon the HTTP request method various `doXXX()` method is invoked by container like `doGet()` to process GET request and `doPost()` to process POST request.

If you remember, to enable Spring MVC, we need to declare the DispatcherServlet from Spring MVC jar into web.xml. This Servlet listens for a URL pattern * as shown in below web.xml, which means all requests are mapped to DispatcherServlet.

Though it is not mandatory, you can have another servlet mapped to another URL if you want to, but if you are using Spring MVC to develop a web application or RESTful web service, it makes sense to pass through all requests via DispatcherServlet.

Here is the web.xml configuration for Spring MVC, you can see that DispatcherServlet is mapped to all request using URL pattern *

```
<web-app>

<!-- The front controller of this Spring Web
application, responsible
for handling all application requests -->
<servlet>
<servlet-name>Spring MVC Dispatcher
Servlet</servlet-name>
<servlet-class>org.springframework.web.servlet.D
ispatcherServlet</servlet-class>
<init-param>
<param-name>contextConfigLocation</param-name>
<param-value>/WEB-INF/config/web-application-
config.xml</param-value>
</init-param>
<load-on-startup>1</load-on-startup>
</servlet>

<servlet-mapping>
<servlet-name>example</servlet-name>
<url-pattern>*</url-pattern>
</servlet-mapping>

</web-app>
```

The URL pattern is important, if the request matches the URL pattern of DispatcherServlet then it will be processed by Spring MVC otherwise not. The DispatcherServlet passes the request to a specific controller depending on the URL requested. How does DispatcherServlet know which request needs to be passed to which controller?

Well, it uses the @RequestMapping annotation or Spring MVC configuration file to find out the mapping of request URL to different controllers. It can also use specific request processing annotations like @GetMapping or @PostMapping. Controller classes are also identified using @Controller and @RestController (in the case of RESTful Web Services) annotations.

For example, the below class is a Controller that will process any request having URI "/appointments". It also has `@GetMapping`, which means that the method will be invoked when a GET request is received for this URL. The method annotated with `@PostMapping` will be invoked if the client sends a POST request to the "/appointments" URI.

```
@Controller
@RequestMapping("/appointments")
public class AppointmentsController {

@GetMapping
public Map get() {
return appointmentBook.
getAppointmentsForToday();
}


@PostMapping
public String add(@Valid AppointmentForm
appointment, BindingResult result) {
if (result.hasErrors()) {
return "appointments/new";
}
appointmentBook.addAppointment(appointment);
return "redirect:/appointments";
}
}
```

After processing the request, the Controller returns a **logical view name** and model to DispatcherServlet and it consults view resolvers until an actual View is determined to render the output. DispatcherServlet then contacts the chosen view e.g. Freemarker or JSP with model data and it renders the output depending on the model data.

This Rendered output is returned to the client as an HTTP response. On it's way back it can pass to any configured Filter as well like Spring Security filter chain or Filters configured to convert the response to JSON or XML.

24. If a user checked in CheckBox and got a validation error in other fields and then he unchecked the CheckBox, what would be the selection status in the command object in Spring MVC? How do you fix this issue?

Since during HTTP post, if the checkbox is unchecked, then HTTP does include a request parameter for checkbox, which means updated selection won't be picked up. You can use the hidden form field, starting with _(underscore) to fix this in Spring MVC. Quite a tricky question to answer if you are not aware of HTTP POST behavior and Spring MVC.

25. What are the different implementations of the View interface

you have used in Spring MVC?

UI based View like JSP, JSTLView,

26. What is the use of DispatcherServlet in Spring MVC?

The `DispatcherServlet` is very important from Spring MVC perspective, it acts as a `FrontController` i.e. all requests pass through it. It is responsible for routing the request to the controller and view resolution before sending the response to the client.

When the Controller returns a Model or View object, it consults all the view resolvers registered to find the correct type of `ViewResolver` which can render the response for clients.

In case of RESTful Web Services, the DispatcherServlet is also responsible for using HttpMessageConverter to represent the response in the JSON, XML, or TEXT format, depending on the content negotiation between Client and Server like if client sends request with HTTP accept header as "`application/json`" then `DispatcherServlet` will ask the `HttpMessageJackson2Converter` to convert the response into JSON format.

27. What is the role of InternalResourceViewResolver in Spring MVC

The **InternalResourceViewResolver** is an implementation of `ViewResolver` in the Spring MVC framework which resolves logical view names like "`hello`" to internal physical resources like Servlet and JSP files e.g. jsp files placed under the WEB-INF folder. It is a subclass of `UrlBasedViewResolver`, which uses "`prefix`" and "`suffix`" to convert a logical view name returned from the Spring controller to map to actual, physical views.

For example, if a user tries to access /home URL and `HomeController` returns "home" then `DispatcherServlet` will consult `InternalResourceViewResolver` and it will use prefix and suffix to find the actual physical view which is integral to a web application.

Like, if the prefix is "/WEB-INF/views/" and the suffix is "`.jsp`" then "`home`" will be resolved to "`/WEB-INF/home.jsp`" by `InternalResourceViewResolver`.

It's also a best practice to put all JSP files inside the WEB-INF directory, to hide them from direct access (e.g. via a manually entered URL). If we put them inside the WEB-INF directory then only controllers will be able to access them.

Even though it's not mandatory that View can only be JSP, it can be JSON also, for example for REST web services, but for the sake of simplicity, we'll take the example of JSP as a view.

By default, `InternalResourceViewResolver`

returns
`InternalResourceView` (i.e. Servlets and JSP)
but it can be configured to return `JstlView` by
using the `viewClass` attribute as shown below:

```
/**
    * Sets the default setViewClass view class to
requiredViewClass: by default
    * InternalResourceView, or JstlView if the
JSTL API is present.
    */
  public InternalResourceViewResolver() {
    Class viewClass = requiredViewClass();
    if (viewClass.equals(InternalResourceView.
class) && jstlPresent) {
      viewClass = JstlView.class;
    }
    setViewClass(viewClass);
  }

  /**
    * This resolver requires
InternalResourceView.
    */
  @Override
  protected Class requiredViewClass() {
    return InternalResourceView.class;
  }
```

The advantage of using `JstlView` is that JSTL
tags will get the Locale and any message
source configured in Spring. This is particularly
important when you are using JSTL tags for
formatting for displaying messages.

28. Difference between @RequestParam and @PathVariable in Spring MVC?

Even though both @RequestParam and @PathVariable are used to extract values from the HTTP request, there is a subtle difference between them, which makes them a useful question from an interview and spring certification point of view. As the name suggests, @RequestParam is used to get the request parameters from URL, also known as query parameters, while @PathVariable extracts values from URI.

For example, if the incoming HTTP request to retrieve a book on topic "Java" is http://localhost:8080/shop/order/1001/receipts?date=12-05-2017, then you can use the @RequestParam annotation to retrieve the query parameter date and you can use @PathVariable to extract the orderId i.e. "1001" as shown below:

```
@RequestMapping(value="/order/{orderId}/
receipts", method = RequestMethod.GET)
public List listUsersInvoices(
@PathVariable("orderId") int order,
 @RequestParam(value = "date", required = false)
Date dateOrNull) {
...
}
```

The required=false denotes that the query parameter can be optional, but the URL must have the same URI.

And here are some key differences between them from an interview perspective.

1) The `@RequestParam` is used to extract query parameters while `@PathVariable` is used to extract data right from the URI.

2) `@RequestParam` is more useful on a traditional web application where data is mostly passed in the query abatements while `@PathVariable` is more suitable for RESTful web services where URL contains values, like `http://localhost:8080/book/9783827319333`, here data, which is ISBN number is part of URI.

3) `@RequestParam` annotation can specify default values if a query parameter is not present or empty by using a defaultValue attribute, provided the required attribute is false.

4) Spring MVC allows you to use multiple `@PathVariable` annotations in the same method, provided, no more than one argument has the same pattern.

29. Difference between @Component, @Service, @Controller, and @Repository annotations in Spring MVC?

All of them are used to auto-detect Spring beans when context scanning is enabled and essentially provide the same functionality with respect to dependency injection.

Their only difference comes in their purpose i.e. `@Controller` is used in Spring MVC to define controllers, which are first Spring bean and then the controller. Similarly, `@Service` is used to annotate classes that hold business logic in the Service layer and `@Repository` is used in the Data Access layer.

Here is a nice summary of what does `@Component`, `@Service`, `@Controller`, and `@Repository` annotation do in Spring Framework:

1. @Component is a generic stereotype for any Spring-managed component or bean.
2. @Repository is a stereotype for the persistence layer.
3. @Service is a stereotype for the service layer.
4. @Controller is a stereotype for the presentation layer (spring-MVC).

30. How do you create a controller in Spring? @Controller vs. @RestController?

A controller is nothing but a class, also known as a bean in Spring terminology. If you are using annotation, then you can create a controller by using `@Controller` annotation.
For RESTful web service, you can also create REST controllers by using the `@RestController` annotation, and in that case, you don't need to use the `@ResponseBody` annotation explicitly to tell Spring how it needs to respond.

That's all about some of the **frequently asked Spring MVC Interview Questions.** If you know answers to these questions mean you have good knowledge of the Spring MVC framework, its different components like DispatcherServlet, handler mappings, Controllers, Views and Model and can explain to anyone.

Sometime, you may get questions from Spring core and Spring security as well, hence it's also advisable to prepare for them. You can find some Spring Security Interview questions here and Some Core Spring questions here.

REST

Hello guys, I have been sharing a lot of REST with Spring tutorials for the last a couple of weeks and today, I am going to share some of the frequently asked Spring and REST interview questions to Java developers applying for Web developer roles.

Since Spring Framework is the most popular and the standard framework for developing Java web application and RESTful Web Services, a good knowledge of Spring core and Spring MVC is expected from any senior Java developer, but if the job description mention about REST and Web Services, you also need to be aware of how to develop RESTful Web Services using Spring Framework.

From Spring 3.1, the framework has been enhanced a lot to support many features needed for RESTFul API out-of-the-box like **HTTPMessageConverter** can convert your HTTP response to JSON or XML by just detecting relevant library in classpaths like Jackson and JAXB.

Spring also provides customized annotations for RESTful Web Services like **@RestController** which can make your Controller REST aware, so that you don't need to do common stuff required by every single REST API like converting the response to JSON.

Good knowledge of Spring Security is also mandatory for developing and security RESTful Web Services in the real world. Since you cannot make life a non-trivial REST API without security, a good knowledge of security basics like HTTP basic authentication, digest authentication, OAuth, and JWT is very important.

Here are a couple of frequently asked questions about using REST Web Services in Spring Framework.

1. What does REST stand for?

REST stands for REpresentational State Transfer, which uses HTTP protocol to send data from client to server like a book in the server can be delivered to the client using JSON or XML.

2. What is a resource?

A resource is how data is represented in REST architecture. By exposing entities as the resource it allows a client to read, write, modify, and create resources using HTTP methods like GET, POST, PUT, DELETE, etc.

3. What are safe REST operations?

REST API uses HTTP methods to perform operations. Some of the HTTP operations which don't modify the resource at the server are known as safe operations e.g. GET and HEAD. On the other hand, PUT, POST, and DELETE are unsafe because they modify the resource on the server.

4. What are idempotent operations? Why

is idempotency important?

There are some HTTP methods e.g. GET which produces the same response no matter how many times you use them e.g. sending multiple GET requests to the same URI will result in the same response without any side-effect hence it is known as idempotent.

On the other hand, the POST is not idempotent because if you send multiple POST requests, it will result in multiple resource creation on the server, but again, PUT is idempotent if you are using it to update the resource.

Even, multiple PUT requests to update a resource on a server will give the same end result.

5. Is REST scalable and/or interoperable?

Yes, REST is Scalable and interoperable. It doesn't mandate a specific choice of technology either at the client or server end. You can use Java, C++, Python or JavaScript to create RESTful Web Services and Consume them at the client end. I suggest you read a good book on REST API e.g. RESTful Web Services to learn more about REST.

6. What are the advantages of the RestTemplate?

The RestTemplate class is an implementation of the Template method pattern in the Spring framework. Similar to other popular template classes like `JdbcTemplate` or `JmsTemplate`, it also simplifies the interaction with RESTful Web Services on the client-side. You can use it to consume a RESTful Web Service very easily as shown in this example.

7. Which HTTP methods does REST use?

REST can use any HTTP methods but the most popular ones are GET for retrieving a resource, POST for creating a resource, PUt for updating the resource and DELETE for removing a resource from the server.

8. What is an HttpMessageConverter in Spring REST?

An `HttpMessageConverter` is a Strategy interface that specifies a converter that can convert from and to HTTP requests and responses. Spring REST uses this interface to convert HTTP responses to various formats e.g. JSON or XML.

Each `HttpMessageConverter` implementation has one or several MIME Types associated with it. Spring uses the "Accept" header to determine the content type the client is expecting.

It will then try to find a registered `HTTPMessageConverter` that is capable of handling that specific content-type and use it to convert the response into that format before sending it to the client.

9. How to create a custom implementation of HttpMessageConverter to support a new type of request/response?

You just need to create an implementation of `AbstractHttpMessageConverter` and register it using the `WebMvcConfigurerAdapter#extendMessage-Converters()` method with the classes which generate a new type of request/response.

10. Is REST normally stateless?

Yes, REST API should be stateless because it is based on HTTP which is also stateless. A Request in REST API should contain all the details required to process i.e. it should not rely on previous or next request or some data maintained at the server end e.g. Sessions. REST specification puts a constraint to make it stateless and you should keep that in mind while designing your REST API.

11. What does @RequestMapping annotation do?

The `@RequestMapping` annotation is used to map web requests to Spring Controller methods. You can map requests based upon HTTP methods like the GET and POST and various other parameters. For examples, if you are developing RESTful Web Service using Spring then you can use produces and consumes property along with media type annotation to indicate that this method is only used to produce or consumers JSON as shown below:

```
@RequestMapping (method = RequestMethod.POST,
consumes="application/json")
public Book save(@RequestBody Book aBook) {
    return bookRepository.save(aBook);
}
```

You can similarly create other handler methods to produce JSON or XML.

12. Is @Controller a stereotype? Is @ RestController a stereotype?

Yes, both `@Controller` and `@RestController` are stereotypes. The `@Controller` is actually a specialization of Spring's `@Component` stereotype annotation. This means that class annotated with `@Controller` will also be automatically be detected by Spring container as part of the container's component scanning process.

And, `@RestController` is a specialization of `@Controller` for RESTful web service. It not only combines `@ResponseBody` and `@Controller` annotation but also gives more meaning to your controller class to clearly indicate that it deals with RESTful requests.

Spring Framework may also use this annotation to provide some more useful features related to REST API development in the future.

13. What is the difference between @ Controller and @RestController?

There are many differences between @ `Controller` and `@RestController` as discussed in my earlier chapter (see the answer) but the most important one is that with @ `RestController` you get the `@ResponseBody` annotation automatically, which means you don't need to separately annotate your handler methods with `@ResponseBody` annotation. This makes the development of RESTful web services easier using Spring.

14. When do you need @ResponseBody annotation in Spring MVC?

The `@ResponseBody` annotation can be put on a method to indicate that the return type should be written directly to the HTTP response body (and not placed in a Model, or interpreted as a view name).
For example:

```
@RequestMapping(path = "/hello", method =
RequestMethod.PUT)
@ResponseBody
public String helloWorld() {
    return "Hello World";
}
```

Alternatively, you can also use `@RestController` annotation instead of `@Controller` annotation. This will remove the need for using @ `ResponseBody` because as discussed in the previous answer, it comes automatically with @ `RestController` annotation.

15. What does @PathVariable do in Spring MVC? Why is it useful in REST with Spring?

It's one of the useful annotations from Spring MVC which allows you to read values from a URI like query parameter. It's particularly useful in case of creating a RESTful web service using Spring because REST resource identifiers are part of URI. This question is normally asked experienced Spring MVC developers e.g. 4 to 6 years of experience.

For example, in the URL `http://myapp.com/` books/101 if you want to extract 101 the id, then you can use `@PathVariable` annotation of Spring MVC.

16. What is the HTTP status return code for a successful DELETE statement?

There is no strict rule with respect to what status code your REST API should return after a successful DELETE i.e it can return 200 Ok or 204 No Content. In general, if the DELETE operation is successful and the response body is empty return 204. If the DELETE request is successful and the response body is NOT empty, return 200

17. What does CRUD mean?

CRUD is a short form of Create, Read, Update and Delete. In REST API, the POST is used to create a resource, GET is used to read a resource, PUT is used to update a resource and DELETE is used to remove a resource from the server. This one is another beginner level Spring MVC questions for 1 to 3 years experienced programmers

18. Where do you need @EnableWebMVC annotation?

The `@EnableWebMvc` annotation is required to enable Spring MVC when Java configuration is used to configure Spring MVC instead of XML. It is equivalent to `<mvc: annotation-driven>` in XML configuration.

It enables support for `@Controller`-annotated classes that use `@RequestMapping` to map incoming requests to handler methods not already familiar with Spring's support for Java configuration,

19. When do you need @ResponseStatus annotation in Spring MVC?

A good question for 3 to 5 years experienced spring developers. The `@ResponseStatus` annotation is required during error handling in Spring MVC and REST. Normally when an error or exception is thrown at the server-side, the web server returns a blanket HTTP status code 500 - Internal server error.

This may work for a human user but not for REST clients. You need to send them a proper status code like 404 if the resource is not found. That's where you can use `@ResponseStatus` annotation, which allows you to send custom HTTP status code along with a proper error message in case of Exception.

In order to use it, you can create custom exceptions and annotate them using `@ResponseStatus` annotation and proper HTTP status code and reason.

When such exceptions are thrown from controller's handler methods and not handled anywhere else, then an appropriate HTTP response with the proper HTTP status code, which you have set, is sent to the client.

For example, if you are writing a RESTful Web Service for a library which provides book information then you can use `@ResponseStatus` to create Exception which returns HTTP response code 404 when a book is not found instead of Internal Server Error (500), as shown below:

```
@ResponseStatus(value=HttpStatus.NOT_FOUND,
reason="No such Book")   // 404
 public class BookNotFoundException extends
RuntimeException {
     // ...
 }
```

If this Exception is thrown from any handler method then HTTP error code 404 with reason "No such Book" will be returned to the client.

20. Is REST secure? What can you do to secure it?

This question is mostly asked with experienced Java programmers e.g. 2 to 5 years experience with both REST and Spring. Security is a broad term, it could mean security of message which is provided by encryption or access restriction which is provided using authentication and authorization. REST is normally not secure but you can secure it by using Spring security.

At the very least you can enable HTTP basic authentication by using HTTP in your Spring security configuration file. Similarly, you can expose your REST API using HTTPS if the underlying server supports HTTPS.

21. Does REST work with transport layer security (TLS)?

TLS or Transport Layer Security is used for secure communication between client and server. It is the successor of SSL (Secure Socket Layer). Since HTTPS can work with both SSL and TLS, REST can also work with TLS.

Actually, REST says anything about Security, it's up to the server which implements that. The same RESTful Web Service can be accessed using HTTP and HTTPS if the server supports SSL.

If you are using Tomcat, you can see here to learn more about how to enable SSL in Tomcat.

22. Do you need Spring MVC in your classpath for developing RESTful Web Service?

This question is often asked Java programmers with 1 to 2 years of experience in Spring. The short answer is Yes, you need Spring MVC in your Java application's classpath to develop RESTful web services using the Spring framework. It's actually Spring MVC which provides all useful annotations e.g. `@RestController`, `@ResponseCode`, `@ResponseBody`, `@RequestBody`, and `@PathVariable`, hence you must spring-mvc.jar or appropriate Maven entry in your pom.xml

That's all about some f**requently asked Spring REST Interview questions** for beginners and experienced Java JEE developers. These questions are also very useful to brush up your knowledge about Spring and REST topics if you are going to take Spring Professional Core Certification.

Spring Boot Intro

If you are preparing for your next Java interview and Job description mentioned about Spring framework, then you should also prepare some **Spring Boot interview questions** to avoid disappointment.

The Spring Boot is now the standard way to use Spring framework for Java development and almost all the companies are moving from the traditional way of using Spring Framework to the more modern Spring Boot way.

Gone are the days, where questions like have you used Spring Boot been asked to the developer. Nowadays interviews expect more knowledge of Spring Boot from candidates and there are reasons for it, which we'll explore in this chapter. Spring Boot aims to simplify Java development with Spring by removing major pain points with respect to configuration, dependency management and ease of development.

As Craig Walls put in Spring boot in Action, **It's probably the best thing that happened to Java after JDK 1.5 release and the introduction of Spring Framework itself some 15 years back.**

It introduces a host of features e.g. starter dependency, auto-configuration, embedded server, Spring Boot CLI, Spring Actuator, Spring Initializer etc to take the Java development with Spring to next level and that's why Spring Boot interview questions are becoming increasingly common in Java interviews.

In order to answer Spring Boot questions with confidence, you not only know what problem Spring Boot solves but also in-depth knowledge of some of its core features like auto-configuration and starter dependencies. These two features eliminate a lot of configuration and setup work from Spring-based Java applications.

1. What is Spring Boot? Why should you use it?

Spring Boot is another Java framework from Spring umbrella which aims to simplify the use of Spring Framework for Java development. It removes most of the pain associated with dealing with Spring e.g. a lot of configuration and dependencies and a lot of manual setups.

Why should you use it? Well, Spring Boot not only provides a lot of convenience by auto-configuration a lot of things for you but also improves the productivity because it lets you focus only on writing your business logic.

For example, *you don't need to set up a Tomcat server* to run your web application. You can just write code and run it as a Java application because it comes with an embedded Tomcat server. You can also create a JAR file or WAR file for deployment based on your convenience.

In short, there are many reasons to use Spring Boot. In fact, it's now the standard way to develop Java applications with Spring framework.

2. What is the advantage of using Spring Boot?

There are several advantages of using Spring Boot the most important one is convenience and productivity. Spring Boot application can be run as a normal Java application like inside the main method. It also comes with starter dependency which means instead of explicitly loading all common libraries, you can load one starter and it will automatically import others.

The Spring CLI features make writing a Spring Boot application even easier using Groovy. You can even write a working Spring Boot application in less than 140 characters, something which you can tweet.

3. What is the difference between Spring Boot and Spring MVC?

Even though both are part of the bigger Spring framework umbrella they are two different frameworks and solve different problems. Spring MVC makes Java web development easier by providing a consistent structure using the Model View Controller design pattern.

On the other hand, Spring Boot aims to simplify the use of Spring Framework including Spring MVC for Java development by adding some painful areas with respect to configuration, dependency management, and running the application.

For example, you need a web-server to run a Spring MVC application but Spring Boot comes with embedded Tomcat or Jetty which can be used to run your Java web application.

4. What is the difference between Core Spring and Spring Boot?

Again, they are two different frameworks but come under the same umbrella of the Spring framework. Core Spring generally refers to Spring container which provides dependency injection and inversion of control, a key feature of Spring framework which promoted writing Java applications in a different way 15 years back. While Spring Boot is now doing the same for the Spring framework, it is promoting a new way to use the Spring framework in the Java project.

5. What are some important features of using Spring Boot?

This is a good subjective question and used by the interviewer to gauge the experience of a candidate with Spring Boot. Anyway, following are some of the important features of Spring Boot framework:

5.1. Starter dependency

This feature aggregates common dependencies together. For example, if you want to develop Spring MVC based RESTful services then instead of including Spring MVC JAR and Jackson JAR file into classpath you can just specify spring-boot-web-starter and it will automatically download both those JAR files. Spring Boot comes with many such starter dependencies to improve productivity.

5.2. Auto-Configuration

This is another awesome feature of Spring Boot which can configure many things for you. For example, If you are developing a Spring web application and Thymeleaf.jar is present on the classpath then it can automatically configure Thymeleaf template resolver, view resolver, and other settings. A good knowledge of auto-configuration is required to become an experienced Spring Boot developer.

5.3. Spring Initializer

A web application which can create initial project structure for you. This simplifies the initial project setup part.

5.4 Spring Actuator

This feature provides a lot of insights of a running Spring boot application. For example, you can use Actuator to find out which beans are created in Spring's application context and which request paths are mapped to controllers.

5.5. Spring CLI

This is another awesome feature of Spring Boot

which really takes Spring development into the next level. It allows you to use Groovy for writing Spring boot applications which means a lot more concise code.

6. What is auto-configuration in Spring boot? How does it help? Why is Spring Boot called opinionated?

There are a lot of questions in this one question itself, but let's first tackle auto-configuration. As explained in the previous example, it automatically configures a lot of things based upon what is present in the classpath.

For example, it can configure `JdbcTemplate` if its present and a `DataSource` bean are available in the classpath. It can even do some basic web security stuff if Spring security is present in the classpath.

Anyway, the point is auto-configuration does a lot of work for you with respect to configuring beans, controllers, view resolvers etc, hence it helps a lot in creating a Java application.

Now, the big questions come, why is it considered opinionated? Well because it makes a judgment on its own. Sometimes it imports things which you don't want, but don't worry, Spring Boot also provides ways to override auto-configuration settings.

It's also disabled by default and you need

to use either `@SpringBootApplication` or `@EnableAutoConfiguration` annotations on the Main class to enable the auto-configuration feature.

7. What is starter dependency in Spring Boot? How does it help?

This question is generally asked as a follow-up of the previous question as it's quite similar to auto-configuration and many developers get confused between both of them. As the name suggests, starter dependency deals with dependency management.

After examining several Spring-based projects Spring guys notice that there is always some set of libraries which are used together e.g. Spring MVC with Jackson for creating RESTful web services. Since declaring a dependency in Maven's `pom.xml` is a pain, they combined many libraries into one based upon functionality and created this starter package.

This not only frees you from declaring many dependencies but also frees you from compatibility and version mismatch issues. Spring Boot starter automatically pulls compatible versions of other libraries so that you can use them without worrying about any compatibility issue.

8. What is the difference between @SpringBootApplication and

@EnableAutoConfiguration annotation?

Even though both are essential Spring Boot applications and used in the Main class or Bootstrap class there is a subtle difference between them. The `@EnableAutoConfiguration` is used to enable auto-configuration but `@SpringBootApplication` does a lot more than that.

It also combines `@Configuration` and `@ComponentScan` annotations to enable Java-based configuration and component scanning in your project.

The @SpringBootApplication is in fact a combination of `@Configuration`, `@ComponentScan` and `@EnableAutoConfiguration` annotations. You can also check Spring Boot MasterClass to learn more about this annotation and it's used.

Also, this Spring Boot question was recently asked to one of my friends in his last interview with a big Investment bank. He was interviewing for a front-office Java web application which uses Spring Boot in the back-end.

9. What is Spring Initializer? why should you use it?

One of the difficult things to start with a framework is initial setup, particularly if you are starting from scratch and you don't have a reference setup or project. Spring Initializer addresses this problem in Spring Boot.

It's nothing but a web application which helps you to create the initial Spring boot project structure and provides a Maven or Gradle build file to build your code.

I highly recommend to use it if you are starting the first time

10. What is a Spring Actuator? What are its advantages?

This is an interesting Spring Boot question and mostly asked on Java roles which also has some support responsibility. Spring Actuator is another cool Spring Boot feature which allows seeing inside a running application.

Yes, you read it correctly. It allows you to see inside an application. Since Spring Boot is all about auto-configuration it makes debugging difficult and at some point in time, you want to know which beans are created in Spring's ApplicationContext and how Controllers are mapped. Spring Actuator provides all that information.

It provides several endpoints like a REST endpoint to retrieve this kind of information over the web. It also provides a lot of insight and metrics about application health like CPU and memory usage, number of threads etc.

It also comes with a remote shell which you can use to securely go inside the Spring Boot application and run some command to expose the same set of data. You can even use JMX to control this behavior at runtime.

Btw, it's important to secure your Spring Actuator endpoints because it exposes a lot of confidential information and a potentially dangerous one-two. For example, by using /showdown endpoint you can kill a Spring Boot application.

But, don't worry. You can use Spring Security to secure Spring Actuator endpoints.

11. What is Spring Boot CLI? What are its benefits?

Spring Boot CLI is a command line interface which allows you to create Spring-based Java applications using Groovy. Since it's used Groovy, it allows you to create Spring Boot applications from the command line without ceremony e.g. you don't need to define getter and setter methods, or access modifiers, return statements etc.
It's also very powerful and can auto-include a lot of libraries in Groovy's default package if you happen to use it.

For example, if you use `JdbcTemplate`, it can automatically load that for you.

12. Where do you define properties in

Spring Boot application?

You can define both application and Spring boot related properties into a file called application. properties. You can create this file manually or you can use Spring Initializer to create this file, albeit empty.

You don't need to do any special configuration to instruct Spring Boot load this file. If it exists in classpath then Spring Boot automatically loads it and configures itself and application code according.

For example, you can use a property to change the embedded server port in Spring Boot, which is also our next question.

13. Can you change the port of the Embedded Tomcat server in Spring boot? If Yes, How?

Yes, we can change the port of Embedded Tomcat Server in Spring Boot by adding a property called `server.port` in the `application.properties` file.

As explained in the previous question, this property file is automatically loaded by Spring Boot and can be used to configure both Spring Boot as well as application code.

If you need an example, you can see this step by step tutorial to change the port of Embedded

Tomcat Server in Spring Boot.

14. What is the difference between an embedded container and a WAR?

The main difference between an embedded container and a WAR file is that you can use a Spring Boot application as a JAR from the command prompt without setting up a web server. But to run a WAR file, you need to first set up a web server like Tomcat which has a Servlet container and then you need to deploy WAR there.

15. What embedded containers does Spring Boot support?

Spring Boot supports three embedded containers: Tomcat, Jetty, and Undertow. By default, it uses Tomcat as embedded containers but you can change it to Jetty or Undertow.

16. What are some common Spring Boot annotations?

Some of the most common Spring Boot annotations are `@EnableAutoConfiguration`, `@SpringBootApplication`, `@SpringBootConfiguration`, and `@SpringBootTest`.
The `@EnableAutoConfiguration` is used to enable auto-configuration on Spring Boot application, while `@SpringBootApplication` is used on the Main class to allow it to run a JAR file. `@`

`SpringBootTest` is used to run unit tests in the Spring Boot environment.

17. Can you name some common Spring Boot Starter POMs?

Some of the most common Spring Boot Start dependencies or POMs are spring-boot-starter, spring-boot-starter-web, spring-boot-starter-test. You can use spring-boot-starter-web to enable Spring MVC in Spring Boot application.

18. Can you control logging with Spring Boot? How?

Yes, we can control logging with Spring Boot by specifying log levels on application.properties file. Spring Boot loads this file when it exists in the classpath and it can be used to configure both Spring Boot and application code.

Spring Boot uses Commons Logging for all internal logging and you can change log levels by adding following lines in the application. properties file:

```
logging.level.org.springframework=DEBUG
logging.level.com.demo=INFO
```

19. Difference between @ SpringBootApplication and @EnableAutoConfiguration annotations in Spring Boot?

The main difference is that `@` `SpringBootApplicaiton` annotation is relatively newer and only available from the Spring Boot 1.2 version while `@EnableAutoConfiguration` is present from the start. Also, `@EnableAutoConfiguration` just enables the auto-configuration feature of the Spring Boot application while `@SpringBootApplication` does three things.

It not only enables auto-configuration but also enables Component scanning and allows you to run your application inside embedded tomcat. You can see the answer chapter for a more detailed explanation.

In short, one is the old way and the other is new. Actually, `@SpringBootApplicaiton` is a combination of three annotations including `@EnableAutoConfiguration`.

20. What is the difference between @ContextConfiguration and @ SpringApplicationConfiguration in Spring Boot Testing?

`@ContextConfiguration` doesn't take full advantage of Spring boot features while loading Spring application context for testing.

21. Where does Spring Boot look for application.properties file by default?

22. How do you define profile specific

property files?

How do you access the properties defined in the property files?

What properties do you have to define in order to configure external MySQL?

How do you configure default schema and initial data?

What is a fat jar? How is it different from the original jar?

What embedded containers does Spring Boot support?

That's all about some of the **common Spring Boot Interview Questions for Java developers**. If you are preparing for a Java development interview where Spring Boot is required as a skill then you should be familiar with these interview questions. They not only help you to do well in your interview but also encourage you to learn key Spring Boot concepts in detail to make the best use of it.

Spring
Boot Auto
Configuration

One of the important features of Spring Boot is the auto-configuration, which makes it possible for the Spring framework to intelligently detect what kind of application you're building and automatically configure the components necessary to support the application's need.

It's built upon the conditional configuration feature introduced in Spring 4 which determines which configuration would be used and which will be ignored at runtime based upon dependencies on application's classpath, environment, and other factors, but with Spring Boot, you don't even need to write the explicit configuration for common scenarios.

Now, let's see some important Auto Configuration related questions for Spring Boot interviews

1. What is Spring Boot auto-configuration?

Spring Boot auto-configuration is a runtime process that considers several factors to decide what Spring configuration should and should not be applied at the application startup-time. Some of its work may be magical to you.

For example, if Spring's `JdbcTemplate` is available on classpath and if there is a DataSource bean then it can auto-configure a `JdbcTemplateBean`.

Similarly, if Spring MVC is on the classpath, Spring's DisapatcherServlet will be configured and Spring MVC will be enabled.

2. How does auto-configuration work? How does it know what to configure?

As explained in the previous example, Spring Boot auto-configuration checks classpath and makes decisions like if a Thymeleaf is present on the classpath then it can configure a Thymelead template resolver, view resolver, and a template engine automatically.

If Spring Data JPA is on the classpath then it can automatically create repository implementations from repository interfaces. Similarly, if Spring Security is present on the classpath then it can configure a very basic web security setup.

It is seriously powerful as it takes more than 200 such decisions every time an application starts up.

3. What are some common Spring Boot annotations?

Some of the common Spring Boot annotations are:

1. @SpringBootApplication

This is the most common Spring Boot annotation and you will find it probably in every single Spring Boot application. Since Spring Boot allows you to execute your Web application without deploying into any web server like Tomcat.

You can run them just like you can run the main class in Java, this annotation is used to annotate the main class of your Spring Boot application. It also enables the auto-configuration feature of Spring Boot.

Here is an example of using the @ SpringBootApplication in Java:

```java
package boot;
import org.springframework.boot.
SpringApplication;
import org.springframework.boot.autoconfigure.
SpringBootApplication;
import org.springframework.web.bind.annotation.
RequestMapping;
import org.springframework.web.bind.annotation.
RestController;

@SpringBootApplication
public class SpringBootDemo {

public static void main(String args[]) {
   SpringApplication.run(SpringBootDemo.class,
args);
}

}

@RestController
class HelloController{

@RequestMapping("/")
public String hello(){
   return "Hello Spring Boot";
```

```
        }

        }
```

This is the simplest example of a RESTful web service you can write using Spring and Java. You can run this like any Java application by right-clicking on the source file and "Run as Java application" in Eclipse. After that, the embedded Tomcat server will start and deploy this RESTful web service.

When you hit the URL `http://localhost:8080/` (the default port for embedded tomcat server inside Spring boot) you will be greeted with "Hello Spring Boot".

Now, coming back to the `@SpringBootApplication` annotation, it's actually a combination of three annotations - `@Configuration`, `@ComponentScan`, and `@EnableAutoConfiguration`.

If you know the `@Configuration` enables Java-based configuration and the class annotated with `@Configuration` can be used to define Spring Beans.

The `@ComponentScan` enables component scanning so that controller or any other component class you create will be automatically discovered and registered with Spring Bean.

And, finally, the `@EnableAutoConfiguration`

enables the auto-configuration feature of Spring Boot which can automatically configure certain Spring features based upon JAR available in Classpath. For example, if H2.jar is present in the classpath, it can configure the H2 in-memory database inside the Spring application context.

By the way, the `@SpringBootApplication` annotation is only available form Spring Boot version 1.1, It wasn't part of Spring Boot's first release and later added because they realize that almost all the applications were annotated with those three annotations (`@Configuration + @ComponentScan, and @EnableAutoConfiguration`).

2. @EnableAutoConfiguration

This is the original Spring Boot annotation which was added to enable the auto-configuration, the flagship Spring boot feature which frees developers from common configuration tasks.

The auto-configuration feature automatically configures things if certain classes are present in the Classpath like if `thymeleaf.jar` is present in the Classpath then it can automatically configure Thymeleaf `TemplateResolver` and `ViewResolver`.

If you are not using `@SpringBootApplication` or running on Spring boot version lower than 1.1 then you can use `@EnableAutoConfiguration` annotates to enable the auto-configuration feature of Spring Boot.

Another thing which is worth knowing about `@EnableAutoConfiguration` is that it allows you to selectively ignore certain classes from auto-configuration using the exclude attribute as shown below:

```
@Configuration
@EnableAutoConfiguration(exclude=
{DataSourceAutoConfiguration.class})
public class SpringBootDemo {
   //.. Java code
}
```

If the class is not on the classpath, you can use the `excludeName` attribute of the `@EnableAutoConfiguration` annotation and specify the fully qualified class name. this Spring Boot annotation is really useful for experienced Spring Boot programmers who think that Spring boot is too opinionated and want to have some control over the auto-configuration feature.

3. @ContextConfiguration

This annotation specifies how to load the application context while writing a unit test for the Spring environment. Here is an example of using `@ContextConfiguration` along with `@RunWith` annotation of JUnit to test a Service class in Spring Boot.

```
@RunWith(SpringJUnit4ClassRunner.class)
@ContextConfiguration(classes=
PaymentConfiguration.class)
public class PaymentServiceTests{

@Autowired
```

```
private PaymentService paymentService;

@Test
public void testPaymentService(){

    // code to test PaymentService class

}

}
```

In this example, `@ContextConfiguration` class instructs to load the Spring application context defined in the `PaymentConfiguration` class.

Btw, even though it does a great job of loading the Spring application context, it doesn't provide full Spring boot treatment.

The Spring Boot applications are ultimately loaded by the `SpringBootApplicaiton` either explicitly or using the `SpringBootServletInitializer`.

This not only leads beans in the Spring application context but also enables logging and loading of properties from external property files like `applicaiton.properties` as well as other Spring Boot features. But, don't worry, there is another annotation that provides all of this and you can use that to write a unit test with Spring boot treatment.

4. @SpringApplicationConfiguration

This is the annotation that addresses the

shortcomings of `@ContextConfiguration` annotation discussed in the previous section. It provides full Spring Boot treatment to your test classes e.g. it not only loads the beans in the Spring application context but also enables logging and loads properties from application.properties file.

Btw, you should always use `@SpringApplicaitonConfiguration` instead of `@ContextConfiguration` for writing unit tests in Spring boot.
Here is an example of using `@SpringApplicatoinConfiguration` annotation in Spring boot:

```
@RunWith(SpringJUnit4ClassRunner.class)
@SpringApplicationConfiguration(classes=
PaymentConfiguration.class)
public class PaymentServiceTests{
    ...

}
```

This is the same example we have seen in the last section but re-written using the `@SpringApplicationConfiguration` annotation this time.

5. @ConditionalOnBean

Spring Boot defines several conditional annotations for auto-configuration like `@ConditionalOnBean` which can be used to apply a configuration if the specified bean has been configured.

`@ConditionalOnMissingBean`

Similarly, you have `@ConditionalOnMissingBean`, which enables the configuration if the specified bean has not already been configured.

`@ConditionalOnClass`

The configuration is applied if the specified class is available on the Classpath.
`@ConditioanlOnMissingClass`

This is the counterpart of the previous annotation. This configuration is applied if the specified class is not present on the Classpath.

`@ConditionalOnExpression`

The Configuration is applied if the given Spring Expression Language (SpEL) expression evaluates to true.

`@ConditionalOnJava`

The Configuration is applied if the version of Java matches a specific value or range of versions.

Apart from these conditional annotations listed here, there are more e.g. `@ConditioalOnJndi`, `@ConditioanlOnProperty`, `@ConditioanlOnResource`, `@`

`ConditionalOnWebApplication`, and `@ConditionalOnNotWebApplication` which works depending upon the presence and absence of some conditions.

4. What does @EnableAutoConfiguration annotation do?

The `@EnableAutoConfiguration` annotation enables auto-configuration in the Spring Boot project. This one line of code literally saves you from writing pages of configurations that would be required otherwise.

5. How does Spring Boot auto-configuration works?

Spring Boot auto-configuration automatically configures a Spring application based on the dependencies present on the classpath. Spring Boot detects classes in the classpath and auto-configuration mechanism will ensure to create and wire necessary beans for you.

You may be thinking how Spring boot knows what to configure? Well it does by detecting JARs and classes in the classpath. For example, if it finds HSQLDB is on your classpath, and you have not manually configured any database connection beans, then we will *auto-configure an in-memory database.*

6. What does @SpringBootApplication do?

The `@SpringBootApplication` annotation is generally used on `Application or Main class` to enable a host of features e.g. Java-based Spring configuration, component scanning, and in particular for enabling Spring Boot's auto-configuration feature.

If you have been using Spring Boot for a long time then you know that earlier we need to annotate our Application class or Main class with quite a lot of annotations to start with like

1. @Configuration to enable Java-based configuration,
2. @ComponentScan to enable component scanning,
3. and @EnableAutoConfiguration to enable Spring Boot's auto-configuration feature,

but now you can do all that by just annotating your Application class with `@SpringBootApplication`.

Btw, this annotation is available from Spring 1.2 onwards which means if you are running on a lower Spring Boot version then you will still need to use the `@Configuration, @ComponentScan,` and `@EnableAutoConfiguration` if you need those features.

Here is a simple example of how to write a Spring Boot application using `@SpringBootApplication` annotation:

```java
import org.slf4j.Logger;
import org.slf4j.LoggerFactory;
import org.springframework.boot.
CommandLineRunner;
import org.springframework.boot.
SpringApplication;
import org.springframework.boot.autoconfigure.
SpringBootApplication;
import org.springframework.web.client.
RestTemplate;


@SpringBootApplication
public class Hello implements CommandLineRunner
{

  private static final Logger log =
LoggerFactory.getLogger(Hello.class);

  public static void main(String args[]) {
    SpringApplication.run(Hello.class);
  }

  @Override
  public void run(String... args) throws
Exception {

    RestTemplate restTemplate = new
RestTemplate();

    Country country = restTemplate.getForObject(
       "http://www.services.groupkt.com/
country/get/iso2code/US",
       Country.class);

    log.info(country.toString());

  }

}
```

The Main class serves two purposes in a Spring Boot application: configuration and bootstrapping. First, it's the main Spring configuration class and second, it enables the auto-configuration feature of Spring Boot application.

7. Does Spring Boot do component scanning? Where does it look by default?

Yes, Spring Boot does component scanning. If you notice, the Main class of a Spring boot application is either annotated with @ `ComponentScan` or @`SpringBootApplication` which is a combination of @`ComponetScan` and two other annotations.

By default Spring Boot look into all the packages under the package containing the Spring Boot application class for components.

The @`ComponentScan` annotation will scan for components in the current package and all its sub-packages. So if your application doesn't have a varying package structure then there is no need for explicit component scanning.

8. How are DataSource and JdbcTemplate auto-configured?

In a Spring Boot application DataSource configuration is specified by external configuration properties in `spring. datasource.*`.

For example, you might declare the following section in `application.properties`:

```
spring.datasource.url=jdbc:mysql://localhost/
test
spring.datasource.username=root
spring.datasource.password=root
spring.datasource.driver-class-name=com.mysql.
jdbc.Driver
```

Similarly, Spring's `JdbcTemplate` and `NamedParameterJdbcTemplate` classes are auto-configured, and you can use `@Autowire` annotation to inject them directly into your own beans.

```
@Component
public class BookDAO{

  private final JdbcTemplate jdbcTemplate;

  @Autowired
  public BookDAO(JdbcTemplate jdbcTemplate) {
    this.jdbcTemplate = jdbcTemplate;
  }
}
```

9. What is the purpose of spring.factories?

This is a special file which powers the auto-configuration feature of Spring Boot application. The `META-INF/spring.factories` specifies all the auto-configuration classes that will be used to guess what kind of application you are running.

Spring Boot checks for the presence of a META-INF/spring.factories file within your application jar. The file should list your configuration classes under the `EnableAutoConfiguration` key, as shown in the following example:

```
org.springframework.boot.
autoconfigure.EnableAutoConfiguration=com.abc.xyz.
autoconfigure.CachingAutoConfiguration
```

10. How do you customize Spring Boot auto configuration?

Spring Boot allows you to customize the auto-configuration as well as create your own custom configuration.

Spring Boot auto configuration is basically a simple **Java configuration class** annotated with @Configuration annotation and enriched with @Conditional* annotations!

- @Configuration : used to specify that a class is a source of bean definitions!
- @Conditional...: used to define some custom conditions on how some beans can be registered in the application context!

Similarly, you can also create your own custom auto-configuration.

11. How to create your own auto-configuration in Spring Boot?

Here are steps to create your own auto-

configuration in Spring Boot:
Create a class annotated as `@Configuration` and register it

```
@Configuration
public class CustomAutoconfiguration {
  // your code
}
```

The next mandatory step is registering the class as an auto-configuration candidate, by adding the name of the class under the key org.springframework.boot. autoconfigure.EnableAutoConfiguration in the standard file resources/META-INF/spring.factories as shown below:

```
org.springframework.boot.
autoconfigure.EnableAutoConfiguration=com.abc.
autocon.CustomAutoConfgiruation
```

12. What are the examples of @ Conditional annotations? How are they used?

As I have said before, the Spring Boot **auto configuration** feature heavily depends on the @ Conditional annotation. Using the `@Conditional` annotation, you can register a bean conditionally based on any specific condition.

For example, you can register a bean when:
* A specific class is present in the classpath
* A Spring bean of a certain type isn't already

registered in the ApplicationContext
- A specific file exists in a location
- A specific property value is configured in a configuration file
- A specific system property is present/absent

Here are some examples of Conditional annotations which you should be aware of:

`@ConditionalOnBean`: Matches when the specified bean classes and/or names are already registered.

`@ConditionalOnMissingBean`: Matches when the specified bean classes and/or names are not already registered.

`@ConditionalOnClass`: Matches when the specified classes are on the classpath.

`@ConditionalOnMissingClass`: Matches when the specified classes are not on the classpath.

`@ConditionalOnProperty`: Matches when the specified properties have a specific value.

`@ConditionalOnResource`: Matches when the specified resources are on the classpath.

`@ConditionalOnWebApplication`: Matches when the application context is a web application context.

That's all about **Spring Boot Auto Configuration based questions.** Auto-configuration is a signature feature of Spring Boot as it takes away the pain for configuring Spring for your application. A good knowledge of how auto-configuration works under the hood and how to use and customize this feature is very important from both interview and Spring certification point of view.

Spring Boot Starter

This is another interesting feature of Spring Boot which makes it easier to select which build and runtime dependencies your application will need by combining commonly needed dependencies.

With Spring Boot starter dependency you can just include one dependency in your pom. xml and rest assured that it will other common dependencies without worrying about the compatible version.

They are also known as starter POMs or simply Spring Boot starter.

1. What is starter dependency in Spring Boot? What is the advantage of it?

The starter dependency feature of Spring Boot solves the problem of dependency management in your project. For example, if you want to build a Java web application using JPA and Thymeleaf template what are the dependencies you will need?

You not only need to figure out a list of dependencies but also their compatible versions. This can be painful and risky if you don't have much experience. Spring Boot solves this problem by introducing "Starter".

Instead of manually adding a library or specifying in Maven or Gradle build file you specify Starter. Each Starter aggregates common and related dependencies like to develop a Spring MVC based application instead of adding all JAR files you can just specify `spring-boot-starter-web starter` in your Maven or Gradle build file and it will import Spring MVC Jar and commonly used libraries like Jackson.

Similarly, if you want to get started using Spring and JPA for database access, include the `spring-boot-starter-data-jpa` dependency in your project.

Internally, Starters are nothing but Maven POM that defines transitive dependencies on other libraries that work together to provide some common functionality.

2. How do you define properties in Spring Boot? Where?

You can define properties in the application. properties file. Spring Boot automatically loads this file and its properties can be used to configure both application and Spring boot.

For example, if you want to change the default port of embedded tomcat server in Spring Boot then you can add server.port = 9000 in this file as shown in this example:

```
$ cat application.properties
server.port = 8080
```

Also, when you use Spring Boot Initializer to create

your project structure, it also creates this file but empty

3. What does @SpringBootApplication annotation do?

This is the main Spring Boot annotation which enables Spring's component-scanning and auto-configuration feature of Spring Boot.

Every Spring Boot application which is not using Spring CLI needs this annotation. Internally, @ `SpringBootApplication` is a combination of three annotations:

Spring's @Configuration which enables Spring's Java-based configuration.

Spring's ComponentScan which enables component scanning so that web controller classes and other components you write are automatically discovered and registered as spring beans in ApplicationContext.

Spring Boot @EnableAutoConfiguration which enables the auto-configuration feature of Spring Boot.

The @SpringBootApplication annotation was introduced in Spring Boot 1. 2, which means in older versions you need to annotate your main class with all of these three annotations.

4. What things affect what Spring Boot

sets up?

Spring Boot's magic depends upon multiple things e.g. annotations, application's classpath, environment, etc. Spring CLI can automatically add packages to Groovy's default package if they are present in the application classpath. Similarly, you can enable auto-configuration by using `@SpringBootApplication` or `@EnableAutoConfiguration` annotations.

5. What does spring boot starter web include?

This is a common starter dependency for building Spring boot based web applications. This dependency uses Spring MVC, REST and Tomcat as a default embedded server. The single **spring-boot-starter-web** dependency transitively pulls in all dependencies related to **web** development. It also reduces the build dependency count. For example, you can just specify `spring-boot-starter-web starter` in your Maven or Gradle build file and it will import Spring MVC Jar and commonly used libraries like Jackson.

6. Can you make your own custom starter dependency?

Yes, it's possible to make your own custom starter dependency in Spring Boot. For example, If you have an internal library for use within your organization, it would be a good practice to also write a starter for it if it's going to be used in

Spring Boot context.

7. What are some common Spring Boot Starter dependencies? Can you name a few?

Here are some of the most common Spring boot starter dependency you need to know as a Java Spring boot developer

1. `spring-boot-starter-web starter` for web applications
2. `spring-boot-starter-data-jpa` for Spring Data JPA
3. `spring-boot-starter-test` for Spring boot testing
4. `spring-boot-starter-parent` for default configurations.
5. `spring-boot-starter-data-ldap` for Spring Data LDAP

8. How do you add a Spring boot starter in your project?

Just like any other dependency, for example, if you are using Maven then you can add following dependency in pom.xml to include Spring boot web starter:

```
<dependency>
    <groupId>org.springframework.boot</groupId>
    <artifactId>spring-boot-starter-web</artifactId>
</dependency>
```

This will add common libraries like e Spring MVC, Tomcat and Jackson in your classpath. Much simpler than adding them individually and worrying about cross-dependency and versions.

9. Which Spring Boot starter will you add to enable Spring boot testing and relevant libraries?

You can use Spring boot Test starter to enable support for Spring boot testing. When you add a Spring boot starter, it will automatically pull common testing libraries like Spring Test, JUnit, Hamcrest, and Mockito in your application classpath.

```
<dependency>
    <groupId>org.springframework.boot</groupId>
    <artifactId>spring-boot-starter-test</artifactId>
    <scope>test</scope>
</dependency>
```

Notice that you don't need to specify the version number of an artifact. Spring Boot will figure out what version to use, all you need to specify is the version of spring-boot-starter-parent artifact.

10. What is Spring Boot Starter Parent?

The spring-boot-starter-parent project is a special starter project – that provides default configurations for your spring boot application and a complete dependency tree to quickly build your Spring Boot project.

It also provides default configuration for Maven plugins such as `maven-failsafe-plugin`, `maven-jar-plugin`, `maven-surefire-plugin`, `maven-war-plugin` etc.

Along with that , it also inherits dependency management from spring-boot-dependencies which is the parent to the spring-boot-starter-parent.

You can start using it in our project by adding this as a parent in your Spring boot project's pom.xml:

```xml
<parent>
    <groupId>org.springframework.boot</groupId>
    <artifactId>spring-boot-starter-parent</artifactId>
    <version>2.4.3</version>
</parent>
```

Once you add this, you don't need to specify the version number of other starter dependencies. Spring Boot will figure out what version to use, all you need to specify is the version of `spring-boot-starter-parent` artifact.

Spring Boot Actuator

If you have used Spring Boot then you may know that Spring Boot is all about convenience and the Spring Boot actuator is one of such features that provides a convenient way to interact with your app live in production.

In fact Actuator is probably the most important feature of a Spring Java application running on production. It provides insights into the inner working of a running Java application which is really important given so much automation.

For example, If you really need to know which beans are configured and how Spring MVC controllers are mapped to request paths then this tool can help you.

The Actuator is mainly used to expose operational and monitoring information about a live Spring boot application like health, metrics, info, dump, env, etc. It provides HTTP endpoints or JMX beans to enable developers and support to interact with them.

When you add spring-boot-starter-actuator maven dependency on the classpath, several endpoints are available for you out of the box, that's what I mean when I say Spring boot is all about developer productivity and convenience. You just add a starter dependency in your Maven or Gradle build file and everything is automatically set up for you.

You can use these endpoints to query your

application status and some important metrics like how many requests have processed, how many of those requests are resulted in errors etc. As a spring boot developer, having a basic knowledge of The actuator is important.

In most of the spring boot interviews, the Interviewer will just ask about what is the actuator, how it works, and some common endpoints which are used often, but if you are preparing for spring professional certification then you need to know this topic in depth.

For example, just knowing how to interact with the spring boot application is not enough, you should also know how to enable/disable some endpoints, you should be able to create your own HealthIndicator as well create your own metrics.

Now, let's see common Actuator interview questions for Spring Boot interviews:

1. What is the Spring Boot Actuator?

It's part of the Spring Boot application that provides deep insights about a running Spring boot application like beans in the Spring application context, auto-configuration decisions, Spring MVC mappings, thread activity, and various applications health metrics.

2. What are the different ways Actuator provides to gain insight into a Spring Boot application?

Spring Boot Actuator provides a couple of ways to retrieve insights and other metrics like it provides REST endpoints, which means you can access metrics over HTTP. It also provides a remote shell to execute a command inside the Spring Boot application and expose much of the same data as the Actuator's endpoints. Also, all of the Actuator's endpoints are exposed as JMX MBeans, which means you can monitor and manage them in runtime using a JMX client like the jConsole.

3. Why do you need to secure Spring Boot Actuator's endpoints?

You need to secure the Spring Boot Actuator's endpoints because it exposes a lot of information from running the Spring Boot application which can be considered sensitive. Some of Spring Boot endpoints like /`shutdown` are also dangerous as a rogue user can shut down the production instance resulting in loss of money and reputation.

4. How do you secure the Spring Boot Actuator's endpoint to restrict access?

Just like Spring MVC application, you can secure the Spring Boot Actuator's endpoints using Spring Security. You can add a Security starter as a build dependency and then security auto-configuration will take care of locking the application, including the Actuator endpoints.

5. What value does Spring Boot Actuator provide?

Spring Boot actuator allows you to monitor and interact with your application which is very important for a production application. Without a spring boot actuator, you need to build your own monitoring and interaction system using JMX, spring boot provides this out-of-box. You can now dynamically change the log level and perform such an operation without restarting your Java and Spring boot applications.

6. What are the two protocols you can use to access actuator endpoints?

Spring Boot allows you to access actuator endpoints using both HTTP and JMX. You can also secure endpoints using Spring Security and in that case, Spring Security's content negotiation strategy is used. You can also enable SSH to access Actuator endpoints.

7. What are the actuator endpoints that are provided out of the box?

The actuator provides a lot of endpoints by default, both sensitive and non-sensitive, but it also allows you to disable sensitive endpoints by configuring them in the application.properties file. Anyway, here are some of the actuator endpoints that are provided out-of-the-box:

- /actuator - provides a hypermedia-based

discovery page for all the other endpoints

- /autoconfig - displays the auto-configuration report in two groups: positive matches and negative matches.
- /beans - displays all the spring beans used in the application
- /configprops - list all the configuration properties that are defined by the @ ConfigurationProperties beans.
- /docs - documentation for all the Actuator module endpoints, requires spring-boot-actuator-docs dependency in pom.xml
- /dump - to get a thread dump of your application
- /env - exposes all the properties from the Spring's ConfigurableEnvironment interface
- /flyway - provides all the information about your database migration scripts; it's based on the Flyway project for database
- /health - shows the health of the application
- /info - displays the public application info
- /logfile - shows the contents of the log file specified by the logging.file property
- /metrics - Various metrics about the app
- /caches - Check available caches

8. What is the info endpoint for? How do you supply data?

Spring Boot Actuator provides an /info endpoint that can provide information about your spring boot application, the best thing about this is that you can customize it as per your application needs. You can add custom information about your application on the application.properties file using the info.app.* properties

Here is an example of how to configure info endpoint:

```
## Configuring info endpoint
info.app.name= My Spring Boot Application
info.app.description=This is my first spring boot
application
info.app.version=1.0.0
```

Spring will automatically add all the properties prefixed with info to the /info endpoint:

```
{
  "app": {
  "description": "This is my first spring boot
application",
  "version": "1.0.0",
  "name": "My Spring Boot Application"
  }
}
```

9. How do you change the logging level of a package using the logger's endpoint?

Spring Boot allows you to view and change the logging level of a spring boot application at runtime using loggers endpoint like `http://localhost:8080/actuator/loggers`. You can connect with this to see all the logging levels provided by the logging framework and then you can also check a particular logger like root

logger as `http://localhost:8080/actuator/loggers/root.`

By the way, Starting with Spring Boot 2.x, most endpoints are not enabled by default, so you will need to enable the /loggers endpoint in our application.properties file as shown below:

```
management.endpoints.web.exposure.include=loggers
management.endpoint.loggers.enabled=true
```

Once enabled, you can change the logging level of a particular package by using an HTTP POST request like this

```
$ curl -i -X POST
        -H 'Content-Type: application/json'
        -d '{"configuredLevel": "DEBUG"}'
http://localhost:8080/actuator/loggers/com.abc.
app.management.logging
```

10. How do you access an endpoint using a tag?

tag is a very useful thing to filter metrics and you should definitely use it to extract meaningful information. You can add any number of tag=KEY:VALUE query parameters to the end of the URL to filter any metric information.

For example, you may know that your application has received 100K requests but you are only interested in requests which resulted in errors like HTTP 404 or HTTP 500 response status.

You can get this information by using the status tag as shown below:

```
$ curl localhost:8081/actuator/metrics/http.
server.requests?tag=status:404
```

11. What are metrics for?

This Spring Boot actuator endpoint shows the metrics information of your spring boot application, where you can determine how much memory it's using, how much memory is free, the uptime of your application, the size of the heap is being used, the number of threads used, and so on.

12. How do you create a custom metric?

Actuator metrics are implemented by Micrometer which means you can also create and publish your custom metric through Micrometer's MeterRegistry.All, you need to do is inject a MeterRegistry wherever you may need to publish counters, timers, or gauges that capture the metrics for your spring boot application.

Here is an example of creating and registering a custom metric in spring-boot:

```
@Component
public class OrderMetrics extends
AbstractRepositoryEventListener {
    private MeterRegistry meterRegistry;

    public OrderMetrics(MeterRegistry
```

```
meterRegistry) {
    this.meterRegistry = meterRegistry;
}

@Override
 protected void onAfterCreate(Order order{
 List items = order.getItems();
 for (Item itm : items) {
    meterRegistry.counter("orderstat", "items",
item.getId()).increment();
 }
 }
}
```

13. What is a Health Indicator in Spring Boot?

A Spring Boot Actuator Health Indicator provides health information of a Spring Boot Application. This health information is accessible at the / health endpoint and can be consumed by monitoring software. By default, multiple Health Indicators are auto-configured.

If you are running a spring boot app with a database app you will see the DB status and by default, you will also see the diskSpace from your system.

If you are running your app, you can go to `http://localhost:8080/` health endpoint to access health status and If you want to learn more check the previous course, it also covers health indicators in good detail.

14. What are the Health Indicators that

are provided out of the box?

Out of the box, Spring Boot registers many HealthIndicators to report the healthiness of a particular application aspect.

Some of those indicators are almost always registered, such as DiskSpaceHealthIndicator or PingHealthIndicator. The DiskSpaceHealthIndicator shows the current state of the disk and the PingHealthIndicator serves as a ping endpoint for the application.

Similarly, Spring Boot also registers some indicators conditionally depending upon which dependencies are available on the classpath or if some other conditions are met

15. What is the Health Indicator status?

It's similar to HTTP status which indicates the health status of your spring boot application and its component, following are some of the common health indicator statuses:

- UP — The component or subsystem is working as expected
- DOWN — The component is not working
- OUT_OF_SERVICE — The component is out of service temporarily
- UNKNOWN — The component state is unknown

The health status affects the HTTP status code of the health endpoint. By default, Spring Boot maps the DOWN, and OUT_OF_SERVICE states to throw a 503 status code. On the other hand, UP and any other unmapped statuses will be translated to a 200 OK status code.

16. What are the Health Indicator statuses that are provided out of the box?

As I said before, some of the health indicators are provided out-of-the-box by spring boot, here are they:

- UP — The component or subsystem is working as expected
- DOWN — The component is not working
- OUT_OF_SERVICE — The component is out of service temporarily
- UNKNOWN — The component state is unknown

17. How do you change the Health Indicator status severity order?

You can use the property management.health. status.order to change the Health Indicator status severity order for your application. For example, if you have a new Status with code FATAL in one of your HealthIndicator implementations.

You may also want to register custom status mappings if you access the health endpoint over HTTP which you can do by adding the following properties in your spring boot application configuration

```
management.health.status.order= BUSY, DOWN, OUT_
OF_SERVICE, UNKNOWN, UP
management.health.status.http-mapping.FATAL=503
```

That's all about the **Spring Boot Actuator Interview Questions and answers**. You can review these questions before you go for any spring boot interview. Since Actuator is an important topic, a good knowledge of Actuator is not only necessary for cracking Java and Spring Boot interviews but also to work effectively in Spring Boot application in your day-to-day life.

Spring Boot CLI

Spring Boot command line really makes it easy to develop Java web applications using Groovy. It takes advantage of Groovy's feature to remove the ceremony associated with writing Java code.

With The Spring CLI, there is no need for accessor methods, access modifiers such as public, private, semicolons, or return keyword. In some cases, you can even get rid of import statements.

On Spring Boot interviews, there are not many questions from this topic but it's good to know about an important Spring Boot feature. More importantly it's great to improve your productivity while working on a Spring Boot project. You can even bootstrap a new project or write your own command for it.

Anyway, let's take a look at the common Spring Boot CLI related questions for Spring Boot interviews:

1. What is Spring Boot CLI?

It's a command-line interface provided by Spring Boot which makes it easy to write Spring Boot applications using Groovy. It leverages the simplicity and convenience offered by auto-configuration and starter dependency and makes it even easier to write Spring boot applications by taking Groovy's power to remove a lot of boiler-plate code from Java. In order to use Spring Boot CLI, you need to install it on your machine.

2. Can you write a Spring application with Groovy?

Yes, Spring Boot CLI makes it possible to write Spring Boot applications in Groovy. It also cut down a lot of noise which comes with writing code in Java.

3. What are the main advantages of the Spring Boot command-line interface (CLI)?

Apart from the convenience of writing Spring application with Groovy, Spring Boot CLI offers the following advantages:

1. It can leverage Spring Boot auto-configuration and starter dependencies.
2. It can detect when certain types are in use and automatically resolve the appropriate dependencies to support those types, though, not all.

CLI has information about which packages some common types belong to like `JdbcTemplate` and common Spring annotations like `@Controller`. If those types are used, it can automatically add those packages to Groovy's default packages at compile time. You can further see

4. What does @Grab annotation do? When to use this?

The @Grab annotation is used to import types which Spring boot CLI cannot resolve automatically. It actually extends @Grab annotation from Gradle, a JAR dependency manager into Groovy, so that, for many frequently used library you can import them by just adding module ID like you can just write `@Grab("h2")` instead of `@Grab("com.h2database:h2:1.4.185")` to import H2 in-memory database and Spring CLI will take care of version, etc.

5. What is Spring Initializer?

Well, the Spring Initializer is a web application that can generate Spring Boot project structure for you. Sometimes creating a project starter is the most difficult thing, especially if you are new to Spring development and Spring Initializer takes care of that. It doesn't generate any code but gives you basic project structure with Maven or Gradle build specification to build your code

6. How does Spring Boot CLI resolve dependencies?

The Spring Boot CLI uses Aether, Maven's dependency resolution engine, to resolve dependencies. The CLI makes use of the Maven configuration found in ~/.m2/settings.xml to configure Aether. The following configuration settings are honored by the CLI:

- Offline
- Mirrors

- Servers
- Proxies
- Profiles
   Activation
   Repositories
- Active profiles

Spring Testing

Testing is an important part of Software development but many people don't pay attention to it only to find bugs in the later stages of development that can be easily avoided by unit testing. When it comes to Java and Spring Boot development, we are lucky to have JUnit, Mockito, and some in-built testing facilities on Spring Framework and Spring Boot for our testing needs.

Since the advent of DevOps, there is an increased focus on automation testing and that's why unit testing and integration testing has become an important topic on Java Interviews and it's essential for Java developers to have in-depth knowledge about how to test a Spring framework and Spring Boot based Java application.

When I first shared my list of Spring Boot Interview Questions, I got a lot of emails to add more interview questions, particularly from Testing and Spring Boot testing topics where I have seen a lot of interest from the interviewers. So, I decided to write a separate chapter containing spring boot testing interview questions.

At that time, many Java developers also asked me to provide answers for Spring and Spring boot testing questions given on the official Spring Certification guide which is also a great resource for anyone preparing for Spring certification and Spring boot interviews.

Since there is a lot of overlap, I have combined all

spring boot testing questions in one chapter. This chapter contains all the answers to Testing and Spring Boot Testing questions from the Spring certification guide as well as some common Spring boot questions.

While many of them are already popular on Spring boot interviews they will also help you to learn Spring boot better and pass the spring certification, if you are aiming to become a certified Spring Developer.

If you have worked on Spring projects then you know that we can use JUnit to test a Spring application and this chapter will show more lights on how to use Spring Test and Spring Boot features to test the interactions between Spring and your code through popular interview questions.

Without any further ado, here is the list of frequently asked Spring and Spring Boot testing interview questions with answers:

1. How to define a testing class in Spring?

Here are the steps needed to define a testing class in Spring application:

- annotate the test class with `@RunWith(SpringJUnit4ClassRunner.class)`
- annotate the class with `@ContextConfiguration` or `@SpringBootTest` in order to tell the runner class where the bean definitions come from

- use `@Autowired` to inject beans to be tested.

That's all you need to do to define a testing class in spring. Super easy? isn't it, that's why I love spring and Spring Boot.

2. Which starter package do you need to test the spring boot application?

To unit test the Spring Boot application you will need to use the spring-boot-starter-test, which imports both Spring Boot test modules as well as JUnit Jupiter, AssertJ, Hamcrest, and a number of other useful libraries. spring-boot-starter-test uses spring-boot-test and spring-boot-test-autoconfigure.

3. What type of tests typically use Spring?

Spring framework provides excellent support for testing, you can write both unit tests and integration tests using Spring and Spring Boot. A unit test is used to test individual classes like controllers while an integration test can be used to test the interaction of multiple units working together. Spring also provides mock objects for unit testing and also provides excellent support for integration tests on the spring-test module.

4. What are the three common Spring boot test annotations?

Three common Spring boot test annotations are `@DataJpaTest`, `@WebMvcTest`, and @

SpringBootTest which can be used to test Spring Data JPA repository, Spring MVC application, and Spring Boot classes.

Spring Boot provides a `@SpringBootTest` annotation, which can be used as an alternative to the standard spring-test `@ContextConfiguration` annotation when you need Spring Boot features.

Spring Boot also provides `@MockBean` annotation that can be used to define a Mockito mock for a bean inside our `ApplicationContext`, which means the mock declared in test class (by using `@MockBean`) will be injected as a bean within the application.

5. How can you create a shared application context in a JUnit integration test?

You can create a shared application context in a JUnit integration test by implementing the `ApplicationContextAware` interface as shown in the following example:

```
@RunWith(SpringRunner.class)
@ContextConfiguration(classes = BookConfiguration.
class)
public class BookBorrowServiceJUnit4ContextTests
implements ApplicationContextAware {
    //some code to test
}
```

6. When and where do you use @ Transactional in testing?

If you remember, the `@Transactional` annotation defines the scope of a single database transaction and a database transaction happens inside the scope of a persistence context. On testing, you can use `@Transaction` annotation at both methods and class level.

At the method level, the annotated test method(s) will run, each in its own transaction. By default, automatically rolled back after completion of the test. You can also alter this behavior by disabling the defaultRollback attribute of `@TransactionConfiguration`.

You can also use `@Transactional` at the class level and in that case, each test method within that class hierarchy runs within a transaction. You can also override this class-level rollback behavior at the method level using the `@Rollback` annotation, which requires a boolean value, `@Rollback(false)`.

7. How are mock frameworks such as Mockito or EasyMock used in Spring Boot?

You can use both Mockito and mock object frameworks like EasyMock to write tests in Spring Boot. Mockito allows you to write tests by mocking the external dependencies with the desired behavior while Mock objects can be used to test specific scenarios.

You can use Mockito in the Spring boot application using either by `@RunWith(MockitoJUnitRunner.class)` to initialize the mock objects or by using MockitoAnnotations.initMocks(this) in the JUnit @ Before method.

You can also use `@MockBean` annotation provided by Spring Boot which can be used to define a new Mockito mock bean or replace a Spring bean with a mock bean and inject that into their dependent beans. Another good thing about this is that If your test uses one of Spring Boot's test annotations (such as `@SpringBootTest`), this feature is automatically enabled.

8. How is @ContextConfiguration used in Spring Boot?

The `@ContextConfiguration` is an important annotation for Spring Boot testing. It is a class-level annotation that is used to load the application context for the integration test. This is defined in the spring-test module.

Here is an example of `@ContextConfiguration` in Spring Boot tests:

```
@RunWith(SpringJUnit4ClassRunner.class)
@ContextConfiguration(classes=BookConfiguration.
class)
public class BookServiceTest {
  @Autowired
  private BookService bookService;
  @Test public void testBookService() {
    Book aBook = bookService.findByTitle("Spring
```

```
Boot in Action");
    assertEquals("Craig Walls", aBook.
getAuthor());
    assertEquals(40, aBook.getPrice());
    }


}
```

This example, it uses BookConfiguration class to create an application context and load bean definitions. if `@ContextConfiguration` is used without any attributes defined, the default behavior of spring boot is to search for a file named {testClassName}-context.xml in the same location as the test class and load bean definitions from there if found.

Spring Boot also provides `@SpringBootTest` annotation, which can be used as an alternative to the standard spring-test `@ContextConfiguration` annotation when you need Spring Boot features.

The annotation works by creating the `ApplicationContext` used in your tests through `SpringApplication` which not only loads the application context but also enables logging and loading of external properties specified in the application.properties or application. yml file, and other features of the Spring Boot framework, which is not loaded or enabled by the `@ContextConfiguration` annotation.

9. How does Spring Boot simplify writing

tests?

Spring boot provides a starter dependency spring-boot-starter-test which loads all-important testing libraries.
For example, the following libraries will be loaded within the test scope:

- JUnit: standard library for writing unit tests in Java
- JSON Path: XPath for JSON
- AssertJ: Fluent assertion library
- Mockito: Java mocking library
- Hamcrest: Library of matcher objects
- JSONassert: Assertion library for JSON
- Spring Test and Spring Boot Test: These are the test libraries provided by the Spring Framework and Spring Boot.

Spring Boot also provides a `@SpringBootTest` annotation, which can be used as an alternative to the standard spring-test `@ContextConfiguration` annotation when you need Spring Boot features.

10. What does @SpringBootTest do? How does it interact with @SpringBootApplication and @SpringBootConfiguration?

The `@SpringBootTest` annotation tells Spring Boot to look for the main configuration class (the one with `@SpringBootApplication`, for instance) and use that to start a Spring application context.

11. When do you want to use @ SpringBootTest annotation?

You can use `@SpringBootTest` annotation whenever you want to test your Spring boot application. For example, you can use @ `SpringBootTest` to verify if the context is loaded or not and if the context is creating your controller or not.

here is an example of using `@SpringBootTest` annotation to check

```
import static org.assertj.core.api.Assertions.
assertThat;
import org.junit.jupiter.api.Test;
import org.springframework.beans.factory.
annotation.Autowired;
import org.springframework.boot.test.context.
SpringBootTest;

@SpringBootTest
public class CheckControllerTest {
    @Autowired
    private BookController controller;

    @Test
    public void contextLoads() throws Exception {
        assertThat(controller).isNotNull();
    }
}
```

You can see we are verifying if the controller is created or not using AssertJ methods.

12. What does @SpringBootTest auto-configure?

Spring Boot provides the `@SpringBootTest` annotation, which can be used as an alternative to the standard spring-test `@ContextConfiguration` annotation when you need Spring Boot features. The annotation works by creating the `ApplicationContext` used in your tests through SpringApplication just like `@SpringApplicaitonConfiguration` does.

13. What dependencies does the spring-boot-starter-test bring to the classpath?

The spring-boot-starter-test adds the following useful testing libraries into classpath:
- JUnit 4: The de-facto standard for unit testing Java applications.
- Spring Test & Spring Boot Test: Utilities and integration test support for Spring Boot applications.
- AssertJ: A fluent assertion library.
- Hamcrest: A library of matcher objects (also known as constraints or predicates).
- Mockito: A Java mocking framework.
- JSONassert: An assertion library for JSON.
- JsonPath: XPath for JSON.

You will generally find these common libraries to be useful when writing tests.

14. How do you perform integration testing with @SpringBootTest for a web

application?

You can either use `@SpringBootTest` to load the full context for integration test or you can use `@WebMvcTest` to only load the web layer interested in loading the whole context.

15. When do you want to use @WebMvcTest? What does it auto-configure?

You can use `@WebMvcTest` annotation for testing the web layer of your Spring Boot application. When you use `@WebMvcTest` instead of `@SpringBootTest` then Spring Boot only instantiates the web layer rather than the whole context.

If your Spring Boot application has multiple controllers then you can even instantiate a particular controller by specifying it as a parameter, for example, `@WebMvcTest(BookController.class)` will only instantiate BookController in your web layer.

16. What are the differences between @MockBean and @Mock annotations?

Both `@Mock` and `@MockBean` are used extensively while writing unit tests in Java and Spring applications. You should use `@Mock` when unit testing your business logic independent of the Spring framework, you can do this by using only using JUnit and Mockito and use @MockBean when you write a test that is backed by a Spring Test Contexts and you want to add or replace a bean with a mocked version of it

17. When do you want @DataJpaTest for? What does it auto-configure?

You can use `@DataJpaTest` annotation to set up an environment with an embedded database to test your database queries against. This is one of the convenient features Spring boot provides to simplify testing.

You can use `@DataJpaTest` to test Spring Data JPA repositories or any other JPA-related components. All you need to do is just add it you our unit test and it will set up a Spring application context:

Here is an example of `@DataJpaTest` annotation in the Spring Boot application:

```
@ExtendWith(SpringExtension.class)
@DataJpaTest

public class OrderEntityRepositoryTest {

    @Autowired
    private DataSource dataSource;
    @Autowired
    private JdbcTemplate jdbcTemplate;
    @Autowired
    private EntityManager entityManager;
    @Autowired
    private OrderRepository orderRepository;
```

```
@Test
public void injectedComponentsAreNotNull(){
  assertThat(dataSource).isNotNull();
  assertThat(jdbcTemplate).isNotNull();
  assertThat(entityManager).isNotNull();
  assertThat(orderRepository).isNotNull();
  }
}
```

Btw, these code examples use the `@ExtendWith` annotation to tell JUnit 5 to enable Spring support. but from Spring Boot 2.1, you don't need to load the SpringExtension because it's automatically included as a meta-annotation in the Spring Boot test annotations like `@DataJpaTest`, `@WebMvcTest`, and `@SpringBootTest`.

18. What is the use of @DirtiesContext annotation while Testing Spring Boot application?

One of the nice features of Spring Test support is that application context is cached between tests. That way, if you have multiple methods in a test case or multiple test cases with the same configuration, they incur the cost of starting the application only once. You can control the cache by using the `@DirtiesContext` annotation.

19. What is the difference between @ContextConfiguration and @ SpringApplicatoinConfiguration in Spring Boot testing?

While both `@ContextConfiguration` and `@SpringApplicatoinConfiguration` annotations can be used to load application context for spring boot testing, there is a subtle difference between them.

While `@ContextConfiguration` loads application context it doesn't take full advantage of useful Spring Boot features. Spring Boot applications are ultimately loaded by either `SpringApplication` (in the case of the JAR) or `SpringBootServletInitializer` (for web applications).

This class not only loads the application context but also enables logging and loading of external properties specified in the application.properties or application.yml file, and other features of the Spring Boot framework, which is not loaded or enabled by the `@ContextConfiguration` annotation.

In short, it's better to use the `@SpringApplicatoinConfiguration` annotations rather than `@ContextConfiguration` for writing an integration test for the Spring boot application.

20. What is the difference between @ContextConfiguration and @SpringBootTest?

This question is also very similar to the previous question. Unlike the `@ContextConfiguration` which just loads spring beans and creates application context for testing without using spring boot features, the `@SpringBootTest` annotation uses SpringApplication behind the scenes to load ApplicationContext so that all the Spring Boot features will be available.

That's all about **Spring Boot Testing Interview Questions and Answers for Java developers.** This chapter not only covers spring boot-specific testing questions but also general Spring framework testing questions. It also answers all the testing-related questions that you will find in the official Spring Certification Exam guide, hence if you are preparing for spring certification, you can also refer to these answers to improve your knowledge about this important topic.

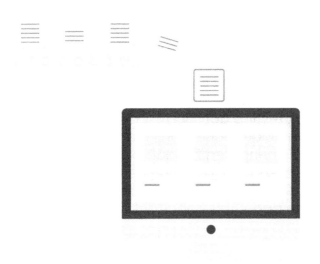

Data Management And JDBC

Who is the main character? Do they have any friends or helpers? Is there someone who challenges the main character? Instead of just naming people, talk about what makes each person memora

1. What is the difference between checked and unchecked exceptions?

Checked and Unchecked Exception are two types of Exception that exist in Java. Though there is no difference in functionality and you can achieve the same thing with either *checked Exception or Unchecked Exception*, there is some difference in the exception handling part. For example, it's mandatory to handle the checked exceptions by either catching them using try and catch blocks or throwing them by using throws clause. For unchecked Exception this is not required.

Checked Exception in Java is all those Exceptions which require being caught and handled during compile time. If Compiler doesn't see a try or catch block handling a Checked Exception, it throws Compilation error. Now Which Exception is checked Exception and Why Checked Exception are introduced in first place? All the Exception which are direct `subClass` of Exception but not inherit `RuntimeException` are Checked Exception.

While doing File Programming in C++ I found that most of the time programmers forgets to close file descriptors , which often result in locking of file on OS level. Since Java was introduced after C++, designers of Java thought to ensure such mistakes are not allowed and resources opened are closed properly. To ensure this they introduced Checked Exception.

If you see most File IO related operations come under IOException which is checked one. Though is a special scenario related to Checked Exception but you can generalize this as, where Java sees an opportunity of failure more, they ensure that programmers provide recovery strategy or at least handle those scenarios gracefully.

2. Why does Spring prefer unchecked exceptions?

The problem with checked exceptions is that they clutter your code with exception handling code and hide the actual business logic. That's why Spring framework uses unchecked exceptions to keep your code clean.

3. What is the Spring data access exception hierarchy?

Spring Data access exception hierarchy starts with org.springframework.dao. DataAccessException, it's an unchecked exception. This exception hierarchy aims to let user code find and handle the kind of error encountered without knowing the details of the particular data access API in use (e.g. JDBC). Thus it is possible to react to an optimistic locking failure without knowing that JDBC is being used.

Also, each data access technology has its own exception types, such as
- **SQLException** for direct JDBC access,
- **HibernateException** used by native Hibernate, or
- **EntityException** used by JPA

Internally, Spring handles technology-specific exceptions and translates them into its own exception hierarchy. The hierarchy is to isolate developers from the particulars of JDBC data access APIs from different vendor.

As this class is a runtime exception, there is no need for user code to catch it or subclasses if any error is to be considered fatal (the usual case).

4. How do you configure a DataSource in Spring?

DataSource interface allows you to obtain connection to external databases in spring based applications. There are many ways to configuring data-source beans, including:

1. Data sources that are defined by a JDBC driver
2. Data sources that are looked up by JNDI.
3. Data sources that connection pool implementation.
4. An embedded database runs as part of your application instead of as a separate database server that your application connects to.

You can configure DataSource using XML configuration or you can also write Java code like below to obtain a DataSource programmatically:

```
@Bean
 public DataSource dataSource() {

    DriverManagerDataSource ds = new
DriverManagerDataSource();
    ds.setDriverClassName("org.h2.Driver");
    ds.setUrl("jdbc:h2:mem:testdb");
    ds.setUsername("sa");
    ds.setPassword("root");
    return ds;
 }
```

5. What is the Template design pattern and what is the JDBC template?

The Template design Pattern is a classic object-oriented design pattern which defines the skeleton of an algorithm in an operation and defer some steps to subclasses. The main benefit of this is that it allows subclasses to redefine certain steps of an algorithm without changing the algorithm's structure.

`JdbcTemplate` is a convenient class in the Spring framework which simplifies the use of JDBC and helps to avoid common errors. It executes core JDBC workflow, leaving application code to provide SQL and extract results. You can use `JdbcTemplate` to execute SQL queries or updates, initiating iteration over `ResultSets` and catching JDBC exceptions and translating them to the generic, more informative exception hierarchy defined in the org.springframework.dao package.

6. What is a callback?

Callbacks are methods which are called by frameworks like SpringFramework at certain events. It allows you to react to those events. For example, you can override callback methods to send welcome email when a new user registers. Spring Framework makes heavy use of callback to allow developers to customize.

7. What are the JdbcTemplate callback interfaces that can be used with queries?

Here are some common JdbcTemplate callback interfaces that can be used with queries.

- `NamedParameterJdbcTemplate` wraps a JdbcTemplate to provide named parameters instead of the traditional JDBC "?" placeholders. This approach provides better documentation and ease of use when you have multiple parameters for an SQL statement.
- `SimpleJdbcInsert` and `SimpleJdbcCall` optimize database metadata to limit the amount of necessary configuration. This approach simplifies coding so that you only need to provide the name of the table or procedure and provide a map of parameters matching the column names.
- `SqlUpdate` and `StoredProcedure` require you

to create reusable and thread-safe objects during initialization of your data access layer. This approach is modeled after JDO Query wherein you define your query string, declare parameters, and compile the query. Once you do that, execute methods can be called multiple times with various parameter values passed in.

- `RowCallbackHandler` interface to extract values from each row of a ResultSet
- `PreparedStatementCallback` is a generic callback interface for code that operates on a PreparedStatement. Allows to execute any number of operations on a single PreparedStatement, for example a single `executeUpdate` call or repeated `executeUpdate` calls with varying parameters.

You can use them depending upon your need. For example, `RowMapper` is often used to convert SQL results to actual Java objects.

8. What is each used for? (You would not have to remember the interface names in the exam, but you should know what they do if you see them in a code sample).

Yes, you can use various `JdbcTemplate` methods to run plain SQL queries. For example, f you want to run an SQL query which runs aggregate functions like `count()`, `avg()`, `max()` and `min()` or just return an integer value then you can use the `queryForInt()` method of `JdbcTemplate` to execute the SQL query as shown in the following example:

```
int total = jdbcTemplate.queryForInt("SELECT
count(*) FROM employee");
```

Similarly, If you want to run an SQL query that returns a value object like String then you can use the `queryForObject()` method of `JdbcTemplate` class. This method takes an argument about what type of class query will return and then converts the result into that object and returns to the caller.

```
String name = jdbcTemplate.queryForObject("SELECT
emp_name FROM employee where emp_id=?",
        new Object[]{103}, String.class);
```

Here is a a list of methods which allows you to run plain SQL queries from Jdbctemplate:

- batchUpdate()
- execute()
- query()
- queryForList()
- queryForObject()
- queryForRowSet()
- update()

You can use them depending upon your need to run SELECT, INSERT, and UPDATE queries.

9. Can you execute a plain SQL statement with the JDBC template?

`JdbcTemplate` acquires and releases the

connection for every method call. A connection is acquired immediately before executing the operation at hand and released immediately after the operation has completed, be it successfully or with an exception thrown.

10. When does the JDBC template acquire (and release) a connection, for every method called or once per template? Why?

`JdbcTemplate` supports querying for any type of object assuming you supplied a RowMapper interface implementation to convert ResultSet into the Java object you want.

It has many overloaded methods for querying the database but mainly you can divide them in:

1. query()
2. queryForObject() if you are expecting only one object
3. queryForMap() will return a map containing each column value as key(column name)/ value(value itself) pairs.
4. queryForList() a list of above if you're expecting more results

11. How do the JdbcTemplate support queries?

Transaction is nothing but an indivisible unit of work. Which either executes in all or none.

Transactions are described in terms of ACID

properties, which are as follows:

- Atomic: all changes to the database made in a transaction are rolled back if any change fails.
- Consistent: the effects of a transaction take the database from one consistent state to another consistent state.
- Isolated: the intermediate steps in a transaction are not visible to other users of the database.
- Durable: when a transaction is completed (committed or rolled back), its effects persist in the database.

Now coming to the difference between a local and global transaction, a local transaction is a simple transaction that is about one single database like transaction associated with a JDBC connection. On the other hand a global transaction means a distributed transaction which is managed by an application server and spreads across many components/ technologies like relational databases and message queues.

For example, consider the case that a record must be persisted in a database ONLY if some message is sent to a queue and processed – if the later fails the transaction must be rolled back.

12. How does it return objects and lists/ maps of objects?

Yes, transaction management is a cross-cutting concern because it spreads across multiple components. It's managed using AOP in Spring. AOP is used to decorate beans with transactional behavior.

This means that when you annotate classes or methods with `@Transactional`, a proxy bean will be created to provide the transactional behavior, and it is wrapped around the original bean in an Around advice that takes care of getting a transaction before calling the method and committing the transaction afterward.

AOP proxies use two infrastructure beans for this:
1. TransactionInterceptor
2. An implementation of
   `PlatformTransactionManager` interface. like:
   1. DataSourceTransactionManager
   2. HibernateTransactionManager
   3. JpaTransactionManager
   4. JtaTransactionManager
   5. WebLogicJtaTransactionManager

The core concept in the Spring transactions world is the **transaction strategy** that is defined by PlatformTransactionManager. This interface is a service provider interface. It has multiple implementations and the one you choose depends on your requirements. When an exception is thrown from within the body of the transactional method, Spring checks the exception type in order to decide if the transaction will commit or rollback.

13. What is a transaction? What is the difference between a local and a global

transaction?

There are two ways to define a transaction in Spring:

1. Declarative way
2. Programmatic way

Declarative way deals with adding some AOP related to transactions to the methods annotated with `@Transactional` or that have some tx-advices defined by XML.

Programmatic way is about using either TransactionTemplate or directly using the `PlatformTransactionManager`. It is also possible to use both declarative and programmatic transaction models simultaneously.

14. Is a transaction a cross-cutting concern? How is it implemented by Spring?

15. How are you going to define a transaction in Spring?

16. What does @Transactional do?

This is a one of the common Spring annotations which allows a bean to have transactional behavior. It relieves the programmer of having to use transactions's `begin()` and `commit()` methods . If you have a method that calls two DAO methods which normally would each have a transaction. ... But if you use `@Transactional` on your method then all those DAO calls will be wrapped in a single `begin()` - `commit()` cycle

17. What is the PlatformTransactionManager?

It is a way to use programmatic transaction management in Spring. If you remember, the Spring framework provides two means of programmatic transaction management.

- Using the transaction template, which is similar to Spring templates, like `JdbcTemplate` and other available templates.
- Using a platform transaction manager, which handles transactions across Hibernate, JDBC, JPA, JMS, etc.

The `PlatformTransactionManager` helps the template to create, commit, or rollback transactions. When using Spring Boot, an appropriate bean of type `PlatformTransactionManager` will be automatically registered, so we just need to simply inject it.

Now transaction template is recommended over using a platform transaction manager because it handles more of the transaction details for us but With `PlatformTransactionManager`, you will have more control over transactions than when using the other programmatic method `TransactionTemplate`. You can decide when to start a transaction, commit, or rollback.

18. Is the JDBC template able to participate in an existing transaction?

Yes, `JdbcTemplate` can participate in an exciting transaction in both declarative and programmatic ways, by wrapping the `DataSource` object using a `TransactionAwareDataSourceProxy`.

This is a proxy for a target `DataSource`, which wraps the target `DataSource` to add awareness of Spring-managed transactions.

19. What is @ EnableTransactionManagement for?

You can use the `@EnableTransactionManagement` annotation with `@Configuration` classes to enable transactional support in Spring Boot. It's similar to `<tx:annotation-driven ../>` tag which enables all infrastructure beans necessary for supporting transactional execution.

Following Components are registered when the `@EnableTransactionManagement` annotation is used:

- A `TransactionInterceptor` which intercept calls to `@Transactional` methods
- A JDK Proxy or AspectJ advice, intercepts methods annotated with `@Transactional`

Another important point to note is that @ `EnableTransactionManagement` only looks for @

`Transactional` on beans **in the same application context they are defined in**. This means that, if you put annotation driven configuration in a `WebApplicationContext` for a DispatcherServlet it only checks for `@Transactional` beans in your **controllers**, and not your services

20. How does transaction propagation work?

Transaction propagation is used to define behavior of the `@Transactional` methods like if they should be executed in an existing or new transaction, or no transaction at all. Propagation is an enum in Spring and here are some common values.

1. Propagation.REQUIRED or @ Transactional(propagation = Propagation. REQUIRED)
    *   Starts a new transaction if there is no transaction.
    *   An existing transaction is kept and the second method call is executed within the same transaction.
    *   If the second method throws an exception that causes rollback, the whole transaction rollback. It doesn't matter if the first transaction handles that exception or not.
    *   Transaction rolls back and throws UnexpectedRollbackException.
2. Propagation.REQUIRES_NEW
    *   always starts a new transaction regardless of whether there is already an active one.

3. Propagation.NESTED
   - there is only one active transaction that spans method calls.
   - only available if your persistence technology is JDBC.
   - it won't work if you are using JPA or Hibernate.
   - JDBC savepoints are used to mark new method calls. When an exception occurs in the second method, the transaction until the last savepoint is rolled back
4. Propagation.MANDATORY
   - An error occurs if there is not an active transaction.
5. Propagation.NEVER
   - An error occurs if there is an active transaction in the system when the method is called.
6. Propagation.NOT_SUPPORTED
   - If there is an active transaction when the method is called, the active transaction is suspended until the end of the method call.
7. Propagation.SUPPORTS
   - the current method works in a transaction if one already exists.
   - Otherwise, the method will work without any transaction.

Here is an example of using Propagation.REQUIRED in Spring:

```
@Service
public class BookServiceImpl implements
BookService {
  @Transactional(propagation = Propagation.
REQUIRED, readOnly= true)
```

```
@Override public Book findByISBN(Long ISBN) {
    return bookRepo.findByISBN(ISBN);
}
}
```

That's all about what is transaction propagation and how does it work.

21. What happens if one @Transactional annotated method is calling another @ Transactional annotated method inside the same object instance?

This is a tricky question and requires good knowledge of Spring AOP to answer correctly. As per the limitation of Spring AOP, a self-invocation of a proxied Spring Bean effectively bypasses the proxy, thus the second method with @Transactional will be executed in the same transaction as the first.

22. Where can the @Transactional annotation be used?

The @Transactional annotation can be used at class level, method level, or interface level. Here is what happens when you @Transaction at class, method and interface level.

Class level:

1. default for all methods of the declaring class and its subclasses
2. method level transactional can override some

attributes

3. does not apply to ancestor classes up the class hierarchy

Method level:

1. You can only use on public methods
2. You can put @Transactional annotation on protected, private or package-visible methods and no error is raised, but the annotated method does not exhibit the configured transactional settings.
3. If you need to annotate non-public methods, consider using AspectJ

Interface:

1. this works only as you would expect it to if you use interface-based proxies

It's recommended that you annotate only concrete classes and methods

23. What is a typical usage if you put it at the class level?

24. What does declarative transaction management mean?• What is the default rollback policy? How can you override it?

The declarative transaction management is preferred way to manage transactions in spring as it handles transaction management for developers. You can use declarative transaction

management by using `@Transactional`
annotation as shown below:

```
@Service
@Transactional
public class BookingService implements
IBookingService {
    public Booking scheduleBooking(Booking
booking) {
        createSlots(booking);
        assignSlotToBooking(booking.getId(),
booking.getSlots());
        return booking;
    }
}
```

This makes your code very easy to maintain and evolve. This is why the Spring team recommends this approach over programmatic transaction management.

Here are key benefits of Declarative Transaction management in Spring:

1. It keeps transaction management out of business logic.
2. It's easy to configure. Use Java annotations or XML configuration files.

When you enable transactions using the above settings Spring begins a new transaction, and when the method returns without any exception it commits the transaction; otherwise, it rolls back. Hence, you don't have to write a single line of transaction demarcation code in your method bodies.

The default rollback policy is to rollback only when a `RuntimeException` is thrown. You can override it by using `rollbackFor` or `noRollbackFor` attribute of `@Transaction` annotation as shown below:

```
@Service
@Transactional(rollbackFor =
SlotNotAvailableException.class)
public class BookingService implements
IBookingService {
    public Booking scheduleBooking(Booking
booking) throws SlotNotAvailableException{
        createSlots(booking);
        assignSlotToBooking(booking.getId(),
booking.getSlots());
        return booking;
    }
}
```

You can also use `rollbackFor` for checked exceptions.

25. What is the default rollback policy in a JUnit test, when you use the @ RunWith(SpringJUnit4ClassRunner. class) in JUnit 4 or @ ExtendWith(SpringExtension.class) in JUnit 5, and annotate your @Test annotated method with @Transactional?

When you use the @ `RunWith(SpringJUnit4ClassRunner.class)` in JUnit 4 or `@ExtendWith(SpringExtension.class)` in JUnit 5, and annotate your `@Test` annotated method with `@Transactional` annotation then

- Test-methods will be executed in a transaction, and will roll back after completion.
- The rollback policy of a test can be changed using the `@Rollback` set to false, `@Rollback(false)`
- `@Commit` indicates that the transaction for a transactional test method should be committed after the test method has completed. You can use `@Commit` as a direct replacement for `@Rollback(false)` to more explicitly convey the intent of the code. Analogous to `@Rollback,` `@Commit` can also be declared as a class-level or method-level annotation.

The @DataJpaTest tests are transactional and rolled back at the end of each test by default. You can disable this default rollback behavior for a single test or for an entire test class by annotating with `@Transactional(propagation = Propagation.NOT_SUPPORTED)`.

Spring Data JPA

Spring Data JPA is an important part of the Spring framework as it makes working with JPA or any JPA implementation like Hibernate easier. Many people think that Spring Data is a replacement of Hibernate but it's not as it's not a JPA implementation. It just provides some convenient abstraction which makes working with any JPA implementation like Hibernate or EclipseLink easier.

Spring Data not only reduces your data access code but also provides you with tons of query flexibility. It also boosts and enhances your data models and gives you enterprise-level features. In short, it's essential for the Java stack.

Questions related to Spring data JPA are always asked in the Spring interview and that's why a Spring developer should always be familiar with Spring Data JPA. One of the common doubts among Java developers is about Spring Data and Hibernate and many of them don't understand the difference between these two essential frameworks.

While Hibernate is a full-fledged JPA implementation, Spring Data JPA provides an additional layer of abstraction or a better API to work with JPA. It's not a JPA implementation, which means you still need to use a JPA implementation like Hibernate but Spring data features like finder methods, and JPQL makes working with databases much easier.

Along with other important concepts, it is also

necessary to know Spring Data JPA to crack Java web developer interviews where Spring Framework skills are required. In this section, we will list the top questions related to Spring JPA and then there are a few more Spring Data questions for you to practice and research on your own.

You can use these questions to revise key Spring Data concepts as well as prepare for both telephonic and face-to-face rounds of Spring developer interviews.

1. What is JPA?

Answer: JPA stands for Java Persistence API. It is a Java specification used to persist data between the relational database and Java objects. It acts as a bridge between object-oriented domain models and relational databases. Since interaction with databases from Java applications is very common, JPA was created to standardize this interaction.

There are many popular JPA implementations available in the Java world like Hibernate and EclipseLink.

2. What are some advantages of using JPA?

Answer: Here are some advantages of Java Persistence API or JPA:
- JPA reduces the burden of interacting with databases.

- Annotation in JPA reduces the cost of creating a definition file.
- It is user-friendly.
- JPA providers help merge applications.

3. What is the Spring data repository?

Answer: Spring data repository is a very important feature of JPA. It helps in reducing a lot of boilerplate code. Moreover, it decreases the chance of errors significantly. This is also the key abstraction that is provided using the Repository interface. It takes the domain class to manage as well as the id type of the domain class as Type Arguments.

4. What is the naming convention for finder methods in the Spring data repository interface?

Answer: This is another key feature of Spring Data JPA API which makes writing query methods really easy. The finder method should use a special keyword, i.e. "find", followed by the name of the variable. For example, findByLastName().

5. Why is an interface not a class?

Answer: Interface is not a class because it does not contain concrete methods. It can contain only abstract methods.

6. Can we perform actual tasks like access, persist, and manage data with

JPA?

Answer: No, we can't because JPA is only a Java specification.

7. How can we create a custom repository in Spring data JPA?

Answer: To create a custom repository, we have to extend it to any of the following interfaces:

a) Repository
b) PagingAndSortingRepository
c) CrudRepository
d) JpaRepository
e) QueryByExampleRepository

8. What is PagingAndSortingRepository?

Answer: PagingAndSortingRepository provides methods that are used to retrieve entities using pagination and sorting. It extends the CrudRepository interface.

9. What is @Query used for?

Answer: Spring Data API provides many ways to define SQL query which can be executed and Query annotations one of them. The @Query is an annotation that is used to execute both JPQL and native SQL queries.

10. Give an example of using @Query

annotation with JPQL.

Answer: Here is an example of @Query annotation from Spring Data Application which returns all active orders from the database:

```
@Query("SELECT order FROM Orders o WHERE
o.Disabled= 0")
Collection<User> findAllActiveOrders();
```

and, here is another example, which returns matching employees from the database

```
@Query("select e from Employee e where se.name =
?1")
List<Employee> getEmployees(String name);
```

11. Can you name the different types of entity mapping.

Answer: one-to-one mapping, one-to-many mapping, many-to-one mapping, and many-to-many mapping.

12. Define entity and name the different properties of an entity.

Answer: An entity is a group of states bundled (or associated) together in a single unit. It behaves like an object. It also becomes a major constituent of the object-oriented paradigm.

13. What is PlatformTransactionManager?

Answer: `PlatformTransactionManager` is an interface that extends `TransactionManager`. It is the central interface in Spring's transaction infrastructure.

14. How can we enable Spring Data JPA features?

Answer: To enable Spring data JPA features, first we have to define a configuration class and then, we can use `@EnableJpaRepositoties` annotation with it. This annotation will enable the features.

15. Differentiate between findById() and getOne().

Answer: The `findById()` is available in CrudRepository while `getOne()` is available in JpaRepository. The `findById()` returns null if record does not exist while the `getOne()` will throw an exception called `EntityNotFoundException`.

16. Are you able to participate in a given transaction in Spring while working with JPA?

Spring Data JPA also allows a configured `JpaTransactionManager` to expose a JPA transaction to JDBC access code that accesses the same DataSource, provided that the registered `JpaDialect` supports retrieval of the underlying JDBC Connection. Out of the box, Spring provides dialects for the EclipseLink, Hibernate and OpenJPA JPA implementations

17. Which PlatformTransactionManager(s) can you use with JPA?

`PlatformTransactionManager` is an important part of Spring transaction management. `PlatformTransactionManager` returns a `TransactionStatus` when you pass a TransactionDefinition to its `getTransaction()` method. In `TransactionDefinition` that is passed we can specify different transaction characteristics like isolation, propagation and timeout.

18. What do you have to configure to use JPA with Spring? How does Spring Boot make this easier?

To enable JPA you need their dependent JAR files in your classpath. Spring boot makes it easy because of auto-configuration and starter dependencies, there are many pre-defined starter packages which you can just in your pom. xml and Spring boot will configure JPA for you.

To enable JPA in a Spring Boot application, you just need the *spring-boot-starter* and *spring-boot-starter-data-jpa dependencies*, as shown below:

```
<dependency>
    <groupId>org.springframework.boot</groupId>
    <artifactId>spring-boot-starter</artifactId>
    <version>2.4.2.RELEASE</version>
</dependency>
<dependency>
    <groupId>org.springframework.boot</groupId>
    <artifactId>spring-boot-starter-data-jpa</
artifactId>
    <version>2.4.2.RELEASE</version>
</dependency>
```

The *spring-boot-starter* contains the necessary auto-configuration for Spring JPA. Also, the *spring-boot-starter-jpa* project references all the necessary dependencies such as hibernate-core.

19. How are Spring Data JPA Repositories implemented by Spring at runtime?

If you have worked with Spring Data JPA repository then you may know that you can add methods like `findByAuthorNameAndTitle()` (assuming authorName and title are fields in the domain object).

Then, Spring provides the implementation by implementing the above repository interface methods at runtime (during the application run). This is implemented using a JDK proxy instance which is created programmatically using Spring's `ProxyFactory` API to back the interface and a `MethodInterceptor` intercepts all calls to the instance and routes the method into the appropriate places, like:

1. If the repository has been initialized with a custom implementation and the method invoked is implemented in that class, the call is routed there.

2. If the method is a query method, the store specific query execution mechanism kicks in and executes the query determined to be executed for that method at startup. For that a resolution mechanism is in place that tries to identify explicitly declared queries in various places (using `@Query` on the method, JPA named queries) eventually falling back to query derivation from the method name.

3. If none of the above apply the method executed has to be one implemented by a store-specific repository base class (`SimpleJpaRepository` in case of JPA) and the call is routed into an instance of that.

20. What type of transaction Management Spring support?

Ans: Following two types of transaction management is supported by spring:

1. Programmatic transaction management
2. Declarative transaction management.

21. How do you call a stored procedure by using the Spring framework?

Spring Framework provides excellent support to

call stored procedures from Java application. In fact, there are multiple ways to call stored procedures in Spring Framework, like you can use one of the `query()` methods from `JdbcTemplate` to call stored procedures, or you can extend abstract class `StoredProcedure` to call stored procedures from Java.

22. What do the JdbcTemplate and JmsTemplate class offer in Spring?

They offer a standard way to use JDBC and JMS API, without writing the boiler code required to work with those API.

That's all about the frequently asked **Spring Data JPA Interview Questions and Answers**. So these were the top 15 questions related to Spring Data JPA. Generally, the Spring data JPA interview questions are more or less related to the above questions listed in this chapter but it's not guaranteed that you will get these questions in a real interview. Instead of mugging these questions I strongly suggest you use them to learn the essential Spring Data JPA concepts better.

These practice questions are also good for Spring professional certification, one of the most in-demand certifications for Java developers.

Spring Cloud

Today is the world of cloud computing and most of the new Java development is happening on Cloud like AWS, GCP, and Azure. That's why it's very important for Java developers to learn about cloud and frameworks and libraries which support cloud-native development in Java, like Spring Cloud from Spring project.

Spring is a powerful framework and probably the most popular Java framework. It is very popular and used widely throughout the world. Spring Cloud is a module provided by Spring that is used to develop cloud-based allocations. In simple words, Spring cloud provides Rapid Application Development (RAD) features to work with Spring.

Because of its popularity and combination of Spring Boot and Spring Cloud for developing cloud-native Java applications and Microservices, you will find many Spring cloud-related questions on Java developer interviews.

If you are preparing for a Java developer interview and your job requires knowledge of Spring Cloud and other Microservice technologies then it makes sense to spend some time learning Spring Cloud and getting yourself familiar with common and frequently asked questions.

Since Spring Cloud is a bit complicated concept, especially for beginners. That is why there is a demand for experienced Spring cloud developers. But as mentioned, it is a complicated concept and interviews related to it have generally tough questions, hence its better to prepare well for this topic

In this chapter, I am going to share the top 15 questions related to Spring cloud for interviews. You can use these questions to not only prepare for the Spring Cloud interview but also to learn and explore essential Spring cloud concepts.

1. Explain Spring cloud? or, What is Spring Cloud?

Answer: Spring cloud is a set of tools that can be used by developers to quickly build some common patterns in distributed systems such as service discovery, configuration management, intelligent routing, etc.

2. What are the common features of Spring cloud?

Answer: Here is a list of some of the most common features of the Spring Cloud framework, which greatly help in developing cloud-native apps and Microservices:

a) Service registration and discovery
b) Routing
c) Service to service calls
d) Distributed and versioned configuration
e) load balancing and circuit breakers

3. Explain load balancing? or What is load balancing?

Answer: Load balancing is a technique used to improve the distribution of workloads across several computing resources, such as a computer cluster, CPUs, network lines, and disk drives.

4. How load balancing is implemented in Spring cloud?

Answer: We can implement load balancing in the Spring cloud using Netflix Ribbon.

5. What is the meaning of Service registration and discovery?

Answer: At the starting of a project, we usually have the entire configurations in the "properties" file. As the project proceeds and more services are developed and deployed, adding them to the properties file becomes complex. It can affect the already deployed services creating problems such as services going down or the location of some might change. Changing the properties manually can create more issues. Service registration and discovery is useful in such situations. The changes can be handled by the service registration and discovery.

6. What is Hystrix?

Answer: Hystrix is a fault-tolerance and latency library designed for isolating points of access to remote systems, third-party libraries, services, stopping cascading failures, and enabling resilience in complex distributed systems where failure is common and cannot be avoided.

7. Explain Netflix feign? Or What is Netflix feign?

Answer: It is a Java to HTTP client binder. It is inspired by JAXRS-2.0, WebSocket, and Retrofit.

8. Why do we use Netflix feign?

Answer: Netflix feign is used to reduce the complexity by binding denominator uniformly to HTTP APIs regardless of the RESTfulness.

9. What is the use of the Spring cloud bus?

Answer: The spring cloud bus provides a helpful feature to refresh configurations across several multiple instances.

10. What are the advantages of Spring cloud?

Answer: Here are key advantages of Spring Cloud
a) Spring cloud helps in resolving complexity associated issues with distributed systems.
b) It provides service discovery which is a very helpful tool.
c) It reduces redundancy.
d) Load balancing is another helpful technique of Spring cloud.

11. What is PCF?

Answer: PCF stands for Pivotal Cloud Foundry. It is an open-source, multi-platform cloud foundry.

12. What is the purpose of the Hystrix circuit breaker?

Answer: The purpose of the Hystrix circuit breaker is to provide the first-page method or any other methods that the method in the first page might be calling and is causing the exception to recover. The chances of exception to recovery may increase because of less load.

13. Name the services that provide service registration and discovery.

Answer: Eureka and zookeeper.

14. Give the benefits of Eureka and Zookeeper?

Answer: Eureka guarantees high availability and usability while Zookeeper guarantees consistency and partition fault tolerance.

15. What is the major difference between Spring Cloud and Spring boot?

Answer: Spring cloud is a microservice management and coordination framework used to integrate and manage individual microservices while Spring boot is used to develop these microservices.

16. What are some common Spring cloud annotations?

Answer: here is a list of some of the most essential Spring cloud annotations for Java developers

1. @EnableConfigServer
2. @EunableEurekaServer
3. @EnableDiscoveryClient
4. @EnableCircuitBreaker
5. @HystricCommand

You can further see the answer for a detailed explanation of these Spring cloud annotations with examples.

That's all about the frequently asked **Spring Cloud Interview Questions for Java and Spring Developers.** You can revise these Spring Cloud questions before attending any Java and Spring framework interview. As I said, Spring cloud is complex, especially for beginners, hence it's also a good idea to spend some time learning Spring cloud itself.

Spring Security

Now that we have seen both Spring core and Spring MVC interview questions, let's explore some frequently asked questions from the Spring Security framework as well because Security is paramount and you will always find using this nice little framework to secret your Java web applications.

Spring Security is one of the most popular security frameworks in the Java world and I strongly believe that every experienced Java developer should learn it. Because of its popularity, there is always some question on Spring Security on Java interviews but there are not enough resources to prepare for that.

In this part, you will find 25+ frequently asked Spring Security Interview Questions for Java Interviews with answers and explanations. You can use this list to not only prepare for a telephonic round of interviews but also for face to face interviews.

Another good thing about these Security questions is that they also answer the Spring security question from the official *Spring Professional Certification Guide*. This means you can also use them to prepare for Spring Certification.

Even if you are not preparing for the Spring Professional certification, you can use questions from this study guide to prepare Spring Security, Spring MVC, and Spring core based upon the topics of Spring Core certification.

After going through these questions I realize that I have already seen many of them on Java Web development interviews that use the Spring framework for building web applications, and that's why I incorporated them into this list of Spring security interview questions.

These questions are good resources to check your existing Spring Security knowledge and at the same time, you can also refresh some important concepts before you appear for any telephonic or face-to-face round of interviews.

I have organized these questions into three different categories, spring-security basics, questions on authentication and authorization, and questions on password encoding and other miscellaneous spring security features.

1. Spring Security Basics Interview questions

In order to effectively use the Spring Security library, it's important for you to understand the basics of Spring security and how spring security works. In this section, we'll see some questions on Spring security architecture and in general how does it work.

1. What is Spring Security?

Spring security is a project under the spring framework umbrella, which provides support for security requirements of enterprise Java projects.

Spring Security, formerly known as aegis security, provides out of box support for creating a login screen, Remember me cookie support, securing URL, authentication provider to authenticate the user from the database, LDAP and in memory, Concurrent Active Session management support, and much more.

In order to use Spring security in a Spring MVC based project, you need to include spring-security.jar and configure it in the `application-Context-security.xml` file, you can name it whatever you want, but make sure to supply this to `ContextLoaderListener`, which is responsible for creating Spring context and initializing dispatcher servlet.

2. What is the delegating filter proxy in Spring Security?

The delegating filter proxy is a generic bean that provides a link between web.xml and application-Context.xml. Spring security uses filters to implement several security related cross-cutting concerns like authentication and authorization.

Since filters need to be declared in the web.xml so that the Servlet container can invoke them before passing the request to the actual Servlet class.

In Spring security, these filters are also Spring bean so that they can take advantage of Spring's dependency injection features, hence they are declared inside the Spring configuration file and a delegating filter proxy (DelegatingFilterProxy) is declared on their behalf on web.xml as filter as shown below:

```xml
<filter>
   <filter-name>springSecurityFilterChain</filter-name>
<filter-class>
     org.springframework.web.filter.
DelegatingFilterProxy
</filter-class>
</filter>

<filter-mapping>
    <filter-name>springSecurityFilterChain</filter-name>
    <url-pattern>/*</url-pattern>
</filter-mapping>
```

At runtime, delegating filter proxy delegates HTTP requests to a bean class for filtering.

3. What are some restrictions on using delegating filter proxy in Spring security?

In order for `DelegatingFilterProxy` to work as expected, there are some rules and restrictions which you need to follow like

1. You must declare a delegating filter proxy to your web.xml as a filter.

2. The target bean must implement the javax.servlet.Filter interface.
3. The target bean must have the same name as that in the filter-name element.
4. You can also specify a "`targetBeanName`" filter init-param in web.xml to specify the name of the target bean in the Spring application context.

4. Do Filter's life-cycle methods like init() and destroy() will be a delegate to the target bean by DelegatingFilterProxy?

No, by default the lifecycle methods defined by the Servlet Filter interface will not be delegated to the target bean, Instead, the Spring application context will manage the lifecycle of that bean. It will be responsible for creating and destroying instances of filter beans.

Though you can enforce invocation of the `Filter.init()` and `Filter.destroy()` lifecycle methods on the target bean by specifying the "targetFilterLifecycle" filter `init-param` as "true". This will let the servlet container manage the filter lifecycle instead of the Spring container.

5. Who manages the life-cycle of filter beans in Spring?

As explained in the previous example, by default Spring container manages the life-cycle of filter beans in Spring i.e. the beans which implements Filter interface and handle request delegated

by delegating Spring proxy, but you can ask
Servlet container to manage their life-cycle
by declaring "targetFilterLifecycle" filter init-
param as "true" on web.xml while declaring the
`DelegatingFilterProxy` filter as shown below:

```
<filter>
    <filter-name>springSecurityFilterChain</filter-
name>
    <filter-class>
        org.springframework.web.filter.
DelegatingFilterProxy
    </filter-class>
</filter>

<filter-mapping>
    <filter-name>springSecurityFilterChain</filter-
name>
    <url-pattern>/*</url-pattern>
</filter-mapping>
```

6. What is the security filter chain in Spring Security?

The Spring Security framework uses a chain of
filters to apply various security concerns like
intercepting the request, detecting (absence of)
authentication, redirecting to the authentication
entry point, or pass the request to authorization
service, and eventually let the request either
hit the servlet or throw a security exception
(unauthenticated or unauthorized).

The `DelegatingFitlerProxy` glues these
filters together and forms the security
filter chain. That's why you see the name

"springsecurityfilterchain" when we declare
DelegatingFilterProxy as a filter in web.xml.

7. What are some predefined filters used by Spring Security? What are their functions and in which order they occurred?

The Spring security filter chain is a very complex and flexible chain of filters. These filter access services such as UserDetailsService and AuthenticationManager to perform their task. Their orders are also important as you may want to check for authentication before authorization.

Here are some of the important filters from Spring's security filter chain, in the order they occur in:

SecurityContextPersistenceFilter - This filter restores Authentication from the JSESSIONID cookie.
UsernamePasswordAuthenticationFilter - This filter performs authentication.

ExceptionTranslationFilter - This filter catches security exceptions from FilterSecurityInterceptor.

FilterSecurityInterceptor - This filter may throw authentication and authorization exceptions.

8. Can you add custom filters in Spring

security's filter chain?

Yes, you can add or replace individual filters with your own logic in Spring's security filter chain. Even though Spring Security provides a number of filters by default, and most of the time, these are enough. You may need to implement new functionality depending upon your project's requirement and this can be done by creating a new filter to use in the chain.

9. How to implement a custom filter in Spring Security?

You can implement a custom filter in Spring security by implementing the org. springframework.`web.filter.GenericFilterBean` class. The `GenericFilterBean` is a simple javax.servlet.Filter implementation which is Spring aware. You can override `doFilter(ServletRequest req, ServletResponse res, FilterChain chain)` to implement your own logic.

10. How to add a custom filter into the Spring Security filter chain?
Depending upon whether you are using Java Configuration or Spring configuration, you can use the following steps to add a custom filter into the security filter chain.

Using XML configuration:

You can add the filter to the chain using the

custom-filter tag and one of the filter aliases like FORM_LOGIN_FILTER, BASIC_AUTH_FILTER to specify the position of your filter. For example, you can add your custom filter after FORM_LOGIN_FILTER as shown below:

```
<beans:bean id="customSpringScurityFilter"
class="CustomSecurityFilter"/>
<http>
  <custom-filter after="FORM_LOGIN_FILTER"
ref="customSpringScurityFilter" />
</http>
```

Here are all attributes to specify exactly where to put your filter in the spring security filter chain:

after - specifies the filter immediately after which a custom filter will be added in the chain.

before - specified the filter before which your custom filter should be placed in the chain.

position - allows you to replace a standard filter in the explicit position with a custom security filter. You can see spring documentation to see the full list of Spring security filter aliases:

Btw, if you are using Java Configuration then you can extend WebSecurityConfigurerAdapter and implement its `configure(HttpSecurity http)` method to put your custom filter in the right place in the spring security filter chain.

11. Is security a cross-cutting concern? How is it implemented internally?

The cross-cutting concern is a concern that is applicable throughout the application and it affects the entire application. For example logging, security, and data transfer are the concerns that are needed in almost every module of an application, hence they are cross-cutting concerns.

Different levels of security are implemented differently like method level security is implemented using AOP. Spring Security framework also uses filters to implement security.

12. What does @ and # is used for in Spring Expression Language (EL)?

The "@" symbol in Spring EL is used to reference a Spring Bean while the "#" symbol in Spring EL allows you to reference a parameter on the method you are securing.

13. Which security annotations are allowed to use SpEL?

The `@PreAuthorize` is one of the most powerful annotations in Spring security which is allowed to use SpEL, but the old @Secured annotation is not allowed to use SpEL like you cannot write `@Secured` ("hasRole('ROLEADMIN')") but you can do `@PreAuthorize`("hasRole('ROLEADMIN')").

14. What is a security context in Spring?

The `SecurityContext` is an interface in the Spring

Security framework which defines the minimum security information associated with the current thread of execution. It provides methods like the `getAuthentication()` which can be used to obtain the currently authenticated principal or an authentication request token. It returns null if no authentication information is available.

2. Spring Security Authentication and Authorization Interview Questions

Now that we have seen many questions based upon Spring security architecture, spring-security filter chain, and other common stuff, it's time to look into another important aspect of Spring security, authentication, and authorization mechanism. In this section, we'll see some frequently asked questions from spring security authentication and authorization functionalities.

15. What are authentication and authorization? Which must come first?

Authentication is a process to verify that the user is the one who he claims to be. It is generally implemented using a username and password. If a user enters the correct username and password then authentication is successful, otherwise, authentication fails.

Authorization provides access control. For example, only the admin can see some pages in a web application. To implement that, the admin must have some admin-related permissions or roles.

If a user becomes admin then those permissions are added to this profile. If you have access to a page it means you are authorized to that page or resources. Obviously, authorization comes after authentication because access can only be provided to genuine users.

16. What is a Principal in Spring Security?

The principal is actually the currently logged in user. You can retrieve security context which is bound to the current thread and as such it's also bound to the current request and its session. The `SecurityContextHolder.getContext()` internally obtains the current `SecurityContext` implementation through a `ThreadLocal` variable. Because a request is bound to a single thread this will get you the context of the current request.

17. Why do you need the intercept-url?

The intercept-url is needed to secure URLs in your Java web application using Spring security. It also defines some sort of authorization, I mean roll or access a user needs to see a page or URL. Most of the web applications using Spring Security only have a couple of **intercept-urls** because they only have very basic security requirements.

You need to have unauthenticated or anonymous access to the login and login-error screens and usually some aspect of the public site, which can be intercepted in a few URL patterns. Then there's often an admin section for admin stuff like creating roles, users, or permissions, and then everything else is ROLE_USER.

Here is one of the examples of **basic Spring security using intercept URL:**

```
<http realm="Contacts Realm" use-
expressions="false">
    <intercept-url pattern="/index.jsp"
access="IS_AUTHENTICATED_ANONYMOUSLY"/>
    <intercept-url pattern="/login.jsp*"
access="IS_AUTHENTICATED_ANONYMOUSLY"/>
    <intercept-url pattern="/admin/*"
access="ROLE_ADMIN"/>
    <intercept-url pattern="/trade/*"
access="ROLE_TRADER"/>
    <intercept-url pattern="/**" access="ROLE_
USER,ROLE_ADMIN,ROLE_TRADER"/>
    <http-basic/>
</http>
```

You can see that index.jsp and admin.jsp are allowed to be accessed without authentication. Anything which has admin in the URL requires ROLE_ADMIN access and any URL with trade in it requires ROLE_TRADER access.

Spring also allows expression-based access control from Spring 3.0 but it is not mandatory, though it gives you more power to implement complex access mechanisms.

18. Why do you need method security?

Security is hard, you often need multiple levels of security to improve the chances to block circumvention attempts. Since method level security is directly coded inside the class, after the AOP augmentation, when you call the method, you'll always call the security check before. Method level security is useful for two main reasons:

1. It provides another layer of security (in addition to other layers)
2. In cases where it's more convenient or logical to have permissions at the method level consider a case where different users can perform the same "direct" actions (so client security isn't relevant). but in some cases, their action may trigger behavior you wish to limit – in this case, method level security may be a relevant solution.

19. Is it enough to hide sections of my output (e.g. JSP-Page)?

Not enough

20. What type of object is typically secured at the method level (think of its purpose, not its Java type).

21. In which order do you have to write multiple intercept-urls?

If you have multiple intercept URLs then you should write them more specific to less specific. Since *intercept-url* patterns are processed in the order in which they appear in the spring security configuration file, it's important that a URL must match with the right pattern.

This becomes even more important when you have wildcards in your URL patterns.
In the following example, any incoming requests that do not match any of the specific patterns would be denied access since `"<intercept-url pattern="/**" access="denyAll" />"` is the last pattern to be matched.

```
<http use-expressions="true">
   <intercept-url pattern="/index.jsp"
access="permitAll" />
   <intercept-url pattern="/secure/admin/**"
access="hasRole('admin')" />
   <intercept-url pattern="/secure/**"
access="isAuthenticated()" />
   <intercept-url pattern="/listAccounts.html"
access="isAuthenticated()" />
   <intercept-url pattern="/post.html"
access="hasAnyRole('supervisor','teller')" />
   <intercept-url pattern="/**" access="denyAll"
/>
   <form-login />
</http>
```

So the most specific patterns should come first, as they are tried in that order. One approach is to **define a whitelist of URLs first then deny everything else.**

22. What do @Secured and @ RolesAllowed do? What is the difference between them?

Th `@Secured` annotation is used to define a list of security configuration attributes for business methods. You can specify the security requirements[roles/permission etc] on a method using the `@Secured` annotation and then only the user with those roles/permissions can invoke that method.

If anyone tries to invoke a method and does not possess the required roles/permissions, an AccessDeniedException will be thrown.

here is a simple example of `@Secured` annotation:

```
@Secured({"ROLE_ADMIN"})
public String showTrades() {
    return "secure/trades";
}
```

The `@Secured` is coming from previous versions of Spring. It has a limitation in that it does not support Spring EL expressions.

It's better to replace `@Secured` annotation with `@PreAuthorize` annotation which supports Spring EL. For example, the above code can be written using `@PreAuthorize` as follows:

```
@PreAuthorize("hasRole('ROLEADMIN')")
public String showTrades() {
    return "secure/trades";
```

```
}
```

On the other hand, `@RolesAllowed` is a JSR 250 annotation, which specifies the security roles permitted to access a method or a couple of methods in an application.

3. Spring Security Password Encoding questions

Now, let's see some Spring security interview questions on password security and protection related topics like hashing and salting, which is also important for Java developers.

23. Does Spring Security support password hashing? What is salting?

One of the common problems of storing passwords on databases is their security. You just can't store passwords as plain text into your database because then anyone who has access to the database would have access to the password of every user. To solve this problem, encrypted passwords are stored in a database and this is known as password hashing.

In cryptography, a salt is random data that is combined with a password before password hashing. This makes a dictionary attack more difficult. This process is known as salting. The hashed version of the password is then stored in a database along with salt.

Btw, some hashing algorithms are not suitable for password hashing, if salt is too small or predictable it's possible to recover passwords by matching random words with salt then comparing the hashed version of output with the data stored in the database.

Yes, Spring Security includes password hashing out of the box. Since version 3.1, Spring Security automatically takes care of salting too. You can use the PasswordEncoder implementation to implement password hashing in Spring security.

24. What is PasswordEncoder?

The PasswordEncoder is an interface in Spring security that provides password encoding or password hashing. It has two methods `encode()` to encode the raw password and `matches()` to verify the encoded password obtained from the database matches the submitted raw password after it too is encoded using the same salt and same hashing algorithm.

25. What are some implementations of PasswordEncoder in Spring Security?

Spring security provides several implementations based upon different hashing algorithms, which you can use in your application. The two important implementations of the new `PasswordEncoder` interface are `BCryptPasswordEncoder` and the confusingly named `StandardPasswordEncoder` based on SHA-256. The BCrypt implementation is the recommended one. There is also a `NoOpPasswordEncoder` which does not encoding. It's intended for unit testing only.

26. How do you control concurrent Sessions on Java web applications using Spring Security?

You can use Spring Security to control the number of active sessions in the Java web application. Spring security framework provides this feature out of the box, and when enabled, a user can only have one active session at a time.

You just need to add a couple of lines of XML in your spring security configuration file and you are done. In order to implement this functionality, you can use the `<concurrency-control>` tag. Similar to this, Spring Security provides lots of Out of Box functionality: a secure enterprise or web application needed for authentication, authorization, session management, password encoding, secure access, session timeout, etc.

Here is sample **spring security Example** of limiting user session in Java web application:

```
<session-management invalid-session-url="/logout.
html">
  <concurrency-control max-sessions="1" error-if-
maximum-exceeded="true" />
</session-management>
```

As you see you can **specify how many concurrent sessions per user is allowed**, a most secure system like online banking portals allows just one authenticated session per user.

The `Max-session` specifies how many concurrent authenticated sessions are allowed and if `error-if-maximum-exceeded` set to true it will flag an error if a user tries to login into another session.

For example, if you try to log in twice from your browser to this spring security application then you will receive an error saying *"Maximum Sessions of 1 for this principal exceeded"*

You can even specify a URL where the user will be taken if they submit an invalid session identifier that can be used to detect session timeout. The session-management element is used to capture the session related stuff.

This is just an example of what Spring security can add to your Java web application. It provides many such advanced and necessary features which can be enabled using some XML tag or annotations.

For example, Spring Security also provides the "remember me" feature which you can use to provide easier access for your users by remembering their login details on their personal computer.

27. How do you set up LDAP Authentication

using Spring Security?

This is a very popular Spring Security interview question as Spring provides out-of-the-box support to connect Windows Active Directory for LDAP authentication and with few configurations in the Spring config file you can have this feature enabled.

There are two ways to implement active directory authentication using LDAP protocol in spring security, the first way is a programmatic and declarative way which requires some coding and some configuration.

On the other hand, the second cond way is an out of box solution from spring security which just requires configuring `ActireDirectoryAuthenticationProvider` and you are done. we will see both approaches but I suggest using the second one because of its simplicity and easy to use a feature.

Add the following configuration into your spring application-context.xml file, I would suggest putting this configuration in a separate **application-context-security.XML** file along with other security-related stuff.

1) Configuring LDAP Server

In order to configure LDAP server, please put following XML snippet into Spring security configuration file:

```
<s:ldap-server
  url="ldap://stockmarket.com"      //ldap url
  port="389"                        //ldap port
  manager-dn="serviceAcctount@sotckmarket.com" //
manager username
  manager-password="AD83DgsSe"                    //
manager password
/>
```

This configuration is self-explanatory but let me give brief summary about manager-in and password, **LDAP authentication on the active directory** or any other LDAP directory is performed in two steps first an LDAP search is performed to locate Dn(Distinguished Name) of the user and then this Dn is used to perform LDAP Bind.
If the bind is successful then user authentication is successful otherwise it fails. **Some people prefer remote compare of password than LDAP bind**, but LDAP bind is what you mostly end up doing.

Most of the Active directory doesn't allow Anonymous Search operation, so to **perform an LDAP search** your service must have an LDAP account which is what we have provided herein `manager-in` and `manager-password.property`.

In **Summary**, now LDAP login will be done in these steps:

1. Your Service or application binds itself with LDAP using manager-dn and manager-password.
2. LDAP search for the user to find UserDn
3. LDAP bind using UserDn

That's the complete LDAP login part. Now, let's move to the next part of configuration LDAP authentication provider.

2. Configuring LDAP Authentication Provider

This section specifies various authentication providers in spring-security here you can see your LDAP authentication provider and we are using `userPrincipalName` to search users inside Microsoft's Active directory.

```
<s:authentication-manager erase-
credentials="true">
<s:ldap-authentication-provider
    user-search-base="dc=stockmarketindia,dc=trad
er"
    user-search-filter="userPrincipalName={0}"
/>

<s:authentication-provider
  ref="springOutOfBoxActiveDirecotry
AuthenticationProvider"/>
</s:authentication-manager>
```

Now a small piece of coding is needed to pass the `userPrincipalName` and authenticate the user.

```
public boolean login(String username, String
password) {
    AndFilter filter = new AndFilter();
    ldapTemplate.
setIgnorePartialResultException(true); // Active
Directory doesn't transparently handle referrals.
This fixes that.
    filter.and(new
EqualsFilter("userPrincipalName", username));
```

```
    return ldapTemplate.
authenticate("dc=stockmarketindia,dc=trader",
            filter.toString(), password);

}
```

line 2 is very important in this program because I spent the whole day figuring out when my application was repeatedly throwing **javax. naming.PartialResultException: Unprocessed Continuation Reference(s)**

you can also use sAMAccountName for the searching user, both `userPrincipalName` and `sAMAccountName` *are unique in the Active Directory.*

What is most important here is that it has to be full name e.g. name@domain like jimmy@stockmarket.com. The `authenticate()` method will return true or false based on a result of the bind operation.

The second approach is much simpler and cleaner because it comes out of the box, you just need to configure LDAP server URL and domain name and it will work like cream.

```
<s:authentication-manager erase-
credentials="true">
    <s:authentication-provider
ref="ldapActiveDirectoryAuthProvider"/>
</s:authentication-manager>

<bean id="ldapActiveDirectoryAuthProvider"
class="org.springframework.security.ldap.
authentication.ad.
```

```
ActiveDirectoryLdapAuthenticationProvider">
    <constructor-arg value="stockmarket.com" />  //
your domain
    <constructor-arg value="ldap://stockmarket.
com/" />  //ldap url
</bean>
```

That's it, done.

28. How to implement Role-Based Access Control (RBAC) using Spring Security?

Spring Security provides a couple of ways to implement Role-based access control like by using `GrantedAuthority`.

Here are the main steps you need to create a RBAC in spring security:

1) Create an Application-specific Authority classes, usually an enum with values like APP_ USER, APP_ADMIN

2) Create an Authority Mapper which will Map LDAP groups to application-specific authority for example if the group in LDAP is "Application Access (Gn)" then mapping that to APP_USER.

3) If you are authenticating against the Active directory then provide your custom Authority mapper to ActiveDirectoryLdapAuthenticationProvider. After successful authentication, it will load all the groups for which authenticated user_id is a member, and map with application-specific

authority.

4) Use application-specific authorities or roles as APP_USER or APP_ADMIN to secure your URL by using

```
<intercept-url pattern="/secure/admin/**"
access="hasRole('APP_ADMIN')"/>
 <intercept-url pattern="/secure/user/**"
access="hasRole('APP_USER')"/>
<intercept-url pattern="/secure/**"
access="isAuthenticated()" /
```

That's all about some of the **frequently asked Spring Security Interview Questions**. These questions are not only great for preparing for Spring job interviews but also for preparing for Spring Professional Certifications. These questions are based upon essential spring security concepts, and a good knowledge of Spring security goes a long way in creating and maintaining a secure Java web and enterprise application.

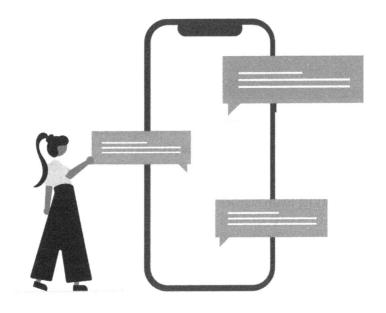

Conclusion

Spring Boot Interview is not easy as you can see there are a lot of topics to master and a lot of concepts to cover. Given the importance of Spring Framework and Spring Boot in Java development, it becomes extremely important for a Java developer to have a strong knowledge of Spring and Spring Boot.

You can use this book in many ways, for example, you can use it to revise frequently asked questions and concepts before you for any telephonic or face-to-face Spring boot interview as well as to get an idea of essential concepts.

The book covers a lot of topics which are normally not exposed in a Java developer job. You have not only learned the basics of Spring and Dependency injection but also learned about key Spring projects like Spring Boot, Spring Security, Spring Data JPA, Spring Cloud and much more.

The areas where you think you need to improve, research more as part of this question. I have learned a lot by doing that in the past. When you research any particular topic or question, your mind is active and eager to learn, whatever you will learn at that time will remain longer in your memory.

Once again, thanks for reading this book and I wish it fulfills your expectations. Don't forget to leave ratings and give feedback as they help us to create more such books and make them even better.

All the best for your Spring Boot interview.

Index

Symbols

@Commit 213
@GetMapping 94
@PostMapping 94
@ResponseStatus 112, 113
@Secured 242, 248

A

abstract 217, 224
Active 176, 235, 253, 254, 255, 256, 257
actuator 9, 160, 161, 163, 164, 165, 166, 167
algorithms 250
AOP 6, 21, 22, 23, 46, 63, 64, 65, 66, 67, 68, 69, 70, 71, 73, 75, 76, 203, 204, 209, 242, 246
ApplicationContext 28, 29, 30, 31, 32, 33, 34, 36, 53, 54, 61, 82, 89, 125, 149, 154, 181, 184, 187, 192
ArrayList 28
AssertJ 180, 185, 186, 187
AuthenticationManager 239
Authorization 243, 244
auto-configuration 9, 18, 117, 118, 121, 122, 123, 124, 125, 128, 130, 133, 134, 135, 137, 138, 140, 142, 143, 145, 146, 147, 148, 150, 154, 155, 161, 162, 164, 173, 174, 221, 222
auto-configure 133, 142, 187, 188, 189

B

Bean Life Cycle 12
bind 135, 254, 256
boilerplate 27, 217

C

checkbox 95
CLI 117, 119, 121, 126, 154, 155, 172, 173, 174, 175

cloud 15, 64, 226, 227, 228, 229, 230, 231
Collections 3
command 95, 126, 128, 162, 173, 174
Constructor injection 18
Container, Dependency Injections and IoC 12
Core spring 12
CreateNewStockAccont 17, 51
cross-cutting 64, 65, 66, 67, 68, 69, 202, 204, 235, 241, 242
CRUD 111, 112
cryptography 249

D

database 46, 137, 142, 153, 164, 168, 175, 182, 189, 196, 198, 201, 202, 216, 219, 235, 249, 250
DELETE 105, 107, 111, 112
Dependency Injection 3, 14, 16, 21
Directory 253, 255, 256
DispatcherServlet 31, 80, 81, 82, 83, 88, 90, 92, 93, 95, 96, 97, 101, 207

E

EnableAutoConfiguration 123, 124, 128, 129, 130, 136, 137, 138, 142, 143, 147, 148, 154, 155
endpoint 125, 126, 162, 164, 165, 166, 167, 168, 169, 170
ExceptionTranslationFilter 239

F

FilterSecurityInterceptor 239
findById() 220
framework 3, 6, 14, 15, 16, 17, 21, 22, 23, 24, 26, 42, 47, 48, 50, 51, 53, 54, 68, 76, 78, 80, 86, 88, 91, 97, 101, 104, 106, 115, 117, 118, 119, 120, 124, 133, 165, 178, 180, 184, 187, 188, 191, 192, 195, 197, 205, 215, 223, 226, 227, 230, 231, 233, 234, 235, 238, 242, 243, 251
FrontController 96
Fundamentals 3

G

getOne() 220
Groovy 119, 122, 126, 155, 173, 174, 175

H

Hamcrest 157, 180, 185, 187
Hystrix 228, 230

I

idempotent 105, 106
integration 21, 33, 34, 54, 178, 180, 181, 183, 187, 188, 191
intercept-url 244, 245, 247, 258
Inversion 14, 16, 22, 78

J

Jackson 104, 120, 123, 153, 155, 157
JAR 18, 22, 29, 69, 91, 118, 120, 121, 128, 137, 153, 175, 191, 221
Java 3, 4, 6, 7, 14, 15, 16, 18, 20, 21, 22, 24, 26, 28, 29, 35,
     50, 51, 56, 59, 62, 64, 69, 70, 73, 76, 78, 79, 80, 91,
     99, 104, 106, 112, 114, 115, 117, 118, 119, 120, 122, 124, 125,
     126, 131, 135, 136, 138, 141, 143, 147, 152, 154, 156, 160,
     163, 171, 173, 174, 178, 185, 187, 188, 192, 215, 216, 218,
     224, 226, 229, 231, 233, 234, 235, 240, 241, 244, 246,
     249, 251, 252, 258, 260
JAXB 104
JdbcTemplate 107, 122, 126, 133, 145, 146, 174, 189, 197,
     198, 199, 200, 201, 205, 206, 224
Jetty 81, 120, 128
JmsTemplate 107, 224
JSON 80, 95, 96, 97, 104, 105, 107, 109, 185, 187
JSP 80, 87, 88, 90, 91, 95, 96, 97, 98, 246
JUnit 34, 138, 157, 178, 179, 180, 181, 183, 185, 187, 188, 190,
     212

L

LDAP 14, 156, 235, 252, 253, 254, 255, 256, 257

LinkedList 28

loading 27, 76, 119, 130, 139, 184, 188, 191

logging 22, 65, 67, 69, 129, 139, 140, 164, 165, 166, 184, 191, 242

M

Mapper 257

Maven 18, 115, 123, 125, 152, 153, 155, 156, 158, 160, 175

metric 166, 167

Microservices 12, 15, 226, 227

Multithreading 3

MySQL 131

O

objects 16, 20, 23, 26, 27, 51, 62, 68, 69, 70, 180, 182, 183, 185, 187, 202, 216

override 20, 38, 56, 122, 182, 198, 209, 210, 212, 240

P

PasswordEncoder 250

PCF 230

Polymorphism 28

POMs 129, 152

POST 92, 94, 95, 105, 106, 107, 108, 109, 112, 166

PreAuthorize 242, 248

prefix 88, 90, 97

Propagation 207, 208, 213

protocol 105, 253

proxy 46, 47, 56, 65, 68, 69, 70, 71, 203, 206, 209, 222, 235, 236, 238

PUT 105, 106, 110, 112

Q

query() 200, 201, 224

R

remote 126, 162, 228, 254
repository 134, 181, 217, 218, 222, 223
REST 6, 9, 12, 97, 101, 104, 105, 106, 107, 108, 109, 111, 112, 113, 114, 115, 125, 155, 162
RESTful 80, 86, 92, 94, 96, 100, 101, 104, 106, 107, 108, 109, 110, 111, 113, 114, 115, 120, 123, 136
return 30, 54, 55, 56, 58, 59, 60, 84, 86, 87, 89, 90, 91, 94, 98, 109, 110, 111, 126, 135, 173, 197, 199, 200, 201, 202, 209, 211, 212, 248, 256
rollback 182, 203, 205, 207, 210, 212, 213
Routing 227
RuntimeException 113, 194, 212

S

Secure Socket Layer 114
security 15, 64, 65, 67, 69, 72, 102, 104, 105, 114, 122, 134, 162, 233, 234, 235, 236, 238, 239, 240, 241, 242, 243, 244, 245, 246, 247, 248, 249, 250, 251, 252, 253, 255, 256, 257, 258
SecurityContextPersistenceFilter 239
servlet 31, 35, 81, 82, 90, 92, 93, 235, 237, 238, 240
sessions 251, 252
setter 17, 18, 19, 20, 21, 126
Spring AOP 6, 22, 23, 46, 65, 69, 70, 71, 75, 76
Spring APIs 3
Spring Aspect-Oriented Programming 12
Spring Boot 1, 3, 4, 5, 6, 7, 8, 9, 12, 14, 16, 18, 34, 76, 117, 118, 119, 120, 121, 122, 123, 124, 125, 126, 127, 128, 129, 130, 131, 133, 134, 135, 136, 137, 138, 139, 140, 142, 143, 145, 146, 147, 148, 149, 150, 152, 153, 154, 155, 156, 157, 158, 160, 161, 162, 163, 164, 165, 166, 167, 168, 169, 171, 173, 174, 175, 178, 179, 180, 181, 182, 183, 184, 185, 187, 188, 189, 190, 191, 192, 221, 226, 260, 261
Spring Boot Actuator 12, 161, 162, 163, 164, 168, 171
Spring Boot Core Concepts 12
Spring Cloud 6, 9, 12, 14, 226, 227, 229, 230, 231, 260
Spring Data JPA 3, 9, 12, 134, 156, 181, 189, 215, 216, 217,

220, 222, 224, 260

Spring Framework 3, 6, 9, 15, 16, 18, 23, 24, 50, 54, 56,
74, 76, 101, 104, 105, 109, 117, 118, 119, 178, 185, 216,
223, 224, 260

Spring MVC 3, 6, 9, 12, 14, 16, 21, 22, 26, 50, 77, 78, 79,
80, 81, 82, 83, 84, 86, 87, 88, 89, 90, 91, 92, 93, 95,
96, 97, 98, 100, 101, 104, 110, 111, 112, 115, 119, 120, 123,
129, 133, 134, 152, 153, 155, 157, 160, 161, 162, 181, 233,
235

Spring Security 4, 12, 14, 15, 95, 102, 104, 126, 134, 162,
163, 233, 234, 235, 238, 239, 240, 242, 243, 244,
249, 250, 251, 252, 253, 257, 258, 260

stereotype 82, 101, 109

suffix 88, 90, 97

T

targetFilterLifecycle 237, 238

Testing 3, 9, 12, 130, 177, 178, 179, 190, 192

Tomcat 3, 81, 91, 92, 115, 118, 120, 127, 128, 135, 136, 155,
157

transaction 22, 182, 202, 203, 204, 205, 206, 207, 208,
209, 210, 211, 213, 220, 221, 223

transaction management 22, 210, 221, 223

Transport Layer Security 114

U

Unchecked 194

unmapped 170

URL 84, 85, 86, 91, 92, 93, 94, 97, 99, 100, 111, 136, 166,
235, 244, 245, 247, 252, 256, 258

UserDetailsService 239

UsernamePasswordAuthenticationFilter 239

V

Vector 28

W

whitelist 247
Windows 253

X

XML 17, 20, 53, 80, 95, 96, 104, 105, 107, 109, 112, 240, 251,
    252, 253